The Nubs

Bite-sized Morsels of Ethics for Daily Life

Molière's 1670 play *Le Bourgeois Gentilhomme* is a send-up on the human failing of trying to appear better than we are. The title is an oxymoron: one can't be a middle-class aristocrat. But M. Jourdain tried his darndest, spending his father's mercantile fortune on tutors to learn the arts of those with natural graces. Jourdain's philosophy tutor ended by just teaching words and revealed the secret that his pupil had actually been speaking prose. Jourdain responds: "My faith! For more than 40 years I have been speaking prose while knowing nothing of it."

This is an apt metaphor for ethics. Ethical behavior, or mangling relationships with others when we weren't being careful, is as constant in human nature as interaction with others. It is to life as speaking or writing is to communication. It is our style.

Getting a tutor to tell us the fancy names for ethical principles is fine, as long as we do not mistake this for being ethical. There will be no test at the Pearly Gates for whether we can spell nonmaleficence. It is not the theory of others we imitate that counts. It is our practice, repeated constantly.

This collection of essays appeared in the *California Dental Association Journal* between September 2009 and August 2019 and is reprinted here with the CDA's generous permission. The common format is to tell a short story about something interesting in human nature and then show that it matters to others in an ethical sense. Ethics is not something we only do when we are thinking about it. I have yet to meet the person who said he or she was choosing to be unethical. It is of marginally passing interest to others what we say about being ethical. "First do it, and then say what you have done." Confucius really did say that in the *Analects*. That is the nub of the matter. Each piece ends by calling out three nubs: three dispositions that others would welcome in us.

The underlying concept of ethics here is acting so that all those affected by our behavior would have no reason to wish our common actions were otherwise. It is about participating in building moral communities and better mutual futures. Sometimes we just need reminders of the amazingly rich opportunities around us to try this out. That is the master nub.

David W. Chambers

Sonoma, California
August 2020

The Nubs: Bite-sized Morsels of Ethics for Daily Life

Published in the United States of America.

FIRST PRINTING August 2020

ISBN: 978-0-578-73384-5 paperback book

Contents

Moral Courage

Polly Powell

Imagine you are on trial, accused of acting morally in your capacity as a dentist. In your heart you know you are ethical, but do you believe there would be enough evidence to get a conviction?

Philosophers usually make a distinction between the academic study of ethics and the practical application of moral behavior. It is something like the difference between architects who design a house and the construction workers who build it. Some very nice plans fail for a lack of resources. Occasionally, the work is less than hoped for due to spotty attention and inadequate skills.

The gap between knowing what to do ethically and doing it is called moral courage. Here are a few examples. Over the years you see the occasional patient treated by a dentist in your community and have watched as the quality decrease: disease conditions are missed, treatment chosen seems difficult to explain, and the technical quality is not up to standard. This troubles you, but you see no clear way to confront the issue.

A family member demands narcotics for pain relief in conjunction with a work injury more than a year ago. You know it is not really right, but it is just easier not to confront the whole family who expect you to cover up. At a component society meeting, a colleague brags about a loophole in the policies of some insurance carriers that permits "perfectly legal" upcoding. You are skeptical and decide that sort of bending the rules is not for you. You mumble something to your colleague about "Well, anything that would level the playing field" and comment later to your friends that "Some people in dentistry are getting pretty commercial, if you know what I mean." In each of these cases, you get high marks for ethics and low marks for moral courage.

There is a phony debate over whether ethical outlook has been entirely formed in youth or at least before dental school. The literature says ethical reasoning skill keeps on developing as long as individuals continue to grow intellectually, with a practical cut off occurring in many cases in the late '30s. But that debate narrows our focus too much. The big challenge is not increasing knowledge of the philosophical principles of ethics or ethical reasoning fluency. What we need is training in communication and assertiveness, professional support groups, peer-review mechanisms, and follow-up on disciplinary actions.

For some, ethics is a spectator sport and we hope our team wins. Getting into the game and actually making a difference to the outcome requires moral courage.

The nub:

❶ Growing an ulcer over a wrong you see or turning it into an opportunity to gloat over your own ethical superiority both are signs of a failure of moral courage.

❷ Confronting wrongs is a skill that can only be learned through active practice.

❸ When broaching moral topics make your words tender, you may have to eat them.

Lemons in Dentistry

Matt Mullin

In the most recent Gallup poll where Americans were asked whether they trust dentists, the profession ranked fifth out of 25, with a 62 percent approval rating. That is the same ranking, but an 11 percent increase in approval over the past quarter century that the survey item has been used.

By contrast, the most recent Gallup data for used car salesmen gives them a 6 percent trust rating. The difference between dentists and used car salesmen is instructive. In 1970, G.A. Akerlof wrote a famous paper called "The Market for 'Lemons.'" His conclusion: "Bad products drive out good products and threaten the very existence of markets, all because current owners know more about the quality of the item to be exchanged than do potential buyers."

It is understood, even if we do not like thinking about it, that there are a few dentists who would count as lemons. Nationally, the rate of disciplined licenses is about 1.5 in 1000, well less than 1 percent. But there may be more whose occasional lapses matter. Most would assume that these lemons sour the public on the profession and hold down the Gallup trust numbers.

How does that come about? A critical part of the process comes from patients' inability to assess the quality of the care they receive. This applies equally to the patients of the most talented and honest dentists and the patients of those who are slipshod or disreputable. The likelihood of getting a dental lemon is determined almost entirely by the dentist and not the patient's skill at detecting lemons. This means that the public cannot be counted on to provide a reasonable check on the spread of lemons.

The next step in the argument is critical: Bad dentists drive out good ones. Thomas Gresham, a London financer, advised Queen Elizabeth I against minting new coins to stop the widespread practice of clipping (shaving off a bit of the edge and collecting these shavings to sell as precious metal while circulating the clipped coins at face value). His reasoning — which is absolutely correct — was that citizens would hoard the new coins and pay their taxes in clipped ones. This phenomenon is called Gresham's Law. Brighter smiles, misleading pricing, and procedures that quack circulate more quickly than fundamental, health-based dentistry.

Think of the reluctance of potential patients to commit to dental care they cannot accurately evaluate as requiring a tax paid to patients to compensate them for the possibility that they will have an unjustifiably negative dental experience. All dentists have to pay the tax.

The final step in the argument is that lemons damage both particular individual buyers and the buying public in general. The market becomes tainted. Patients demand more of all dentists now in order to protect themselves from the possibility of the few bad actors.

The nub:

1. Inform and educate patients so they can recognize good dentistry.
2. Challenge the lemons that will move the cost of bad dentistry from you to them.
3. Be a champion for the profession and comprehensive, continuous, competent, compassionate dentistry.

What Is Trust Worth?

Steve Dininno

Human interactions are never perfectly articulated. He is late for the first meeting; she gave you the wrong information; they needed a little extra time to pay; the dentist said the sensitivity would stop soon. What a stupid, low-level, uptight world we would deal for ourselves if we failed to extend the trust necessary to grease the inevitable and random irregularities of interpersonal relations. Imagine a monetary system that constrained credit.

Individuals in America exhibit a range of trust as a basic personality characteristic. Some folks are trusters and some are not. Research has shown that those who by nature trust more are happier, wealthier, and less likely to be the victims of misplaced trust. Trust is a skill and those who practice get good at it.

Trust means voluntarily making oneself vulnerable with the anticipation of greater rewards from cooperation than are likely from noncooperation. Sometimes the anticipated benefit from trust is a greater reward. Sometimes the anticipated benefit from trust is reducing the cost of transactions.

The phrase "I trust him about as far is his self-interests extend" makes perfect sense. Mutual self-interest, rather than presumed altruism or a sense of fairness, is the correct basis for trust. When agreements benefit all parties concerned, they can be counted on to be adhered to. These are referred to as self-enforcing agreements. They make possible things that could not be accomplished alone; they smooth out the random irregularities in social intercourse; and they reduce the costs of making contracts, monitoring them, and paying third parties.

Self-enforcing, mutually beneficial interactions are one of the hot new areas in moral philosophy. These contractarian theories of ethics turn out to successfully predict human behavior and explain us at our best. They also help identify where things can go wrong. The best places to look for abuses of trust are deception, coercion, and reneging. The con game, which depends on an assumption of both trust and greed, works by appealing to unrealistic self-interests. A dentist would be unethical in the trust sense of the term if he or she deceived the patient regarding what work needed to be done, offered only some treatment alternatives (coercion), or changed the conditions of the treatment plan midtreatment. Patients could violate trust by misstating their health condition or financial condition, threatening suit over things that did not happen, or failing to pay for care.

The concepts of what is ethical and what is legal in dentistry are sometimes blurred. One way to distinguish them is to ask how much trust is involved. Legal settlements, even including arbitration in some cases, bleed all the trust out of the relationship. Ethics puts trust back in.

The nub:

❶ Don't expect relationships to last if there is not something of value in it for each party.

❷ High trust increases the size of the pie; low trust decreases it — no matter how it is divided.

❸ Practice the skill of trust building.

Screw-ups

Dan Hubig

Every dental office is well-stocked with a supply of screw-ups. We teach students to distinguish between those that are unavoidable by a competent and well-motivated dentist (called "bad outcomes") and those that reasonably could have been avoided (called "bad work"). Peer-review committees, lawyers, and malpractice carriers make such distinctions; patients not so much.

The overriding rule, the essence of the American Dental Association's Ethics Code, is that patients must be made aware of their oral conditions. This is a requirement for describing the condition and explaining its significance. The matter of accepting responsibility, justifying what has been done, or otherwise owning the problem is a separate matter.

Reports are beginning to appear in the medical literature that lawsuits can be reduced in frequency and in cost when physicians acknowledge and express regret over unwelcome outcomes, regardless of fault.

The major categories of response to unwelcome outcomes include expression of regret, apology, excuses and justification, offers of reparation, diagnosis and explanation, encouragement or acceptance of legal remedies, arbitration, promise making, and bluffing, or doing nothing. The question is, which ones work best in which situations? If the unwelcome outcome is an unforeseeable result, despite good intentions and good procedures or if it is a result discussed in informed consent chosen by the patient, expression of regret, denial of responsibility, diagnosis and explanation, and perhaps promising to work out a new approach, are good strategies.

If the unwelcome outcome is a result of negligence, poor skill, misjudgment, or other form of isolated incompetence in the eyes of the patient, the correct response is expression of regret, diagnosis and communication, offers of reparation, and above all, an apology. An apology involves the twin components of regret and acceptance of responsibility. The goal in this situation is to repair the level of trust between the dentist and patient. Legal or arbitration responses will not do this. Engaging the patient in diagnosing, even tentatively what is at stake in correcting the problem, is an excellent strategy. Research has shown that positive gestures are magnified where the concern is competence.

The opposite happens when the patient perceives that the issue is the dentist's integrity: cutting corners, lack of informed consent, overtreating, etc. In such situations, negative information is weighed excessively. Dentists should not apologize but should consider denial of responsibility, excuses and justification, and legal settlement. I am not so much offering advice for bad actors to beat the rap as altering those who make the occasional, well-intended misstep that patients will interpret the strategies of the dentist with poor motives as evidence that the dentist lacks integrity.

The nub:

1. Never let another dentist be the first to tell a patient that there was an unwelcome event in their mouth.
2. Explain and offer to help when unwelcome outcomes occurred by chance.
3. Apologize if it is reasonable for the patient to believe that the unwelcome even was caused by a slip of competence.

Club Ethics

Deborah Zemke

When greeted in public with the question, "How are you," the proper response is "I'm fine. How are you?" To say that you are "superb" is presumptuous; it is an imposition to begin a list of ailments and complaints. Violating a confidence would be terribly bad form for a friend and unforgivable, and perhaps even legally actionable in a priest, health care provider, or attorney. On the other hand, in politics and the entertainment industries, failure to pass on the well-placed leak would jeopardize one's status in the network.

Club ethics regulate the way we behave in groups. Politicians can be elected while in jail, serving sentences for bribery, while others have their re-elections sabotaged for voting their conscience against the party caucus. In extreme cases, gang members must demonstrate conspicuous flaunting of the public good (as in tagging), and mafioso or CIA agents might kill to demonstrate their good ethical status. What we are dealing with is cases where a positive bond between members and the group demands behavior that is independent of or in some cases antithetical to ethics generally.

Professional ethicists have focused almost exclusively on the nature of moral acts. It also matters who is affected by moral behavior and the style in which it is done. I have heard stories of dentists whose treatment of patients was so alarming that the profession vigorously sought to curb their practices, only to be blocked or equivocated by the legal system. But when the minor restraints imposed by justice were tampered with, the same dentist gets the "contempt of court" book thrown at them. It matters which club's rules are violated.

The challenge of club ethics exists in the American Dental Association Code, most notably in Section 4C: "Patients should be informed of their oral health status without disparaging comment about prior service." This standard from the section labeled "Professional Conduct" is at odds with the statement in the "Ethics" section that "the benefit of the patient (is the dentist's) highest goal." There is a conflict here between club ethics and ethical responsibility to the public.

In many years of leading case discussions with students and practitioners, there have been a surprising number who place the club ethic higher than the general one. Several practitioners who have been officers in organized dentistry have strongly stated there are no circumstances whatsoever that justify challenging the work of colleagues. One told me recently, "Patients come and go; I have to live with my colleagues throughout my career."

These same practitioners find it troublesome that dental students pretty rigorously enforce the club ethic of not ratting on colleagues who are known to cheat in dental school.

The nub:

1. In ethics, it matters what is done, but also whom it is done to and how.
2. Following the norms of one's group is often easier and more highly rewarded than being ethical in general.
3. Choose your friends carefully: they define what it means to be good.

Dr. Congeniality

Matt Mullin

There is a belief circulating that being ethical is the consolation prize for practitioners who cannot be successful. Most famously, the German philosopher Friedrich Nietzsche, in his *Genealogy of Morals,* argued that morality functions as a cloak of justification for those who are not strong enough to compete in the real world.

It is easy to think of instances where a dentist pockets more money charging for work that is unnecessary or was never performed. But such acts do not prove that material success trumps ethics. If it did, all the world would be cutthroat competition. It is the pattern that matters: Which is the better policy, generally ethical competition or competition that abuses ethics?

Research clearly favors the ethical organization. The Malcolm Baldrige National Quality Award has been given for about 20 years to organizations — including hospitals and medical group practices — and includes ethics and community orientation among its criteria. Winners of the Baldrige Prize consistently outperform the market. Business school researchers have summarized the central findings of studies showing that ethical firms, including those that create positive cultures, outperform their competitors in the following areas: productivity, innovation, quality, customer retention, employee loyalty, and profitability. Perhaps paradoxically, ethical firms extend their lead over these preoccupied with material success in difficult circumstances, such as the airlines following Sept. 11 and the recent economic downturn.

Researchers have reported that scores on tests of moral judgment predict good clinical judgment of physicians, high scores on moral reasoning and related to high clinical performance of dental students. There are several studies showing that moral skills are associated with fewer malpractice claims among medical practitioners.

Let's be as fair as we can about the evidence for the association between ethics and success. Although it demonstrates that such a connection can be found in general, it is not inevitable. Further, there is no way to determine for certain which way the causal arrow is pointing. It is possible that individuals and organizations that are successful can afford the luxury of being moral. It is quite plausible that faulty ethics symptomatic of low competence in the material sense. All of this said, the smart money would be on pursuing a career grounded in both excellence in dentistry and moral strength: they are certainly not incompatible.

The discussion above has one major qualification: it is only true when the prevailing ethic in society is positive toward morality. The strong association between ethics and success would not be likely in a prison environment, among gangs and groups of con artists, or even in some industries. When the prevailing culture is winner take all, the ethical practitioner is only eligible for the Dr. Chump Prize.

The nub:

1. Never use ethics as an excuse for not having succeeded as a dentist.
2. Never use the goal of success as an excuse for skimping on ethics.
3. Build a general culture of ethics as a protection against being caught as a chump.

Enduring Patients

Matt Mullin

"Patient" is not a term used to describe a person in need of oral health care or medical treatment, generally. Many Americans suffer the pain of tooth loss or oral cancer and have no charts in any dental office. On the opposite side, there are Americans who attend the dentist regularly to hear that there is nothing amiss in their mouths or to get their teeth a few shades whiter.

A patient is an individual who has agreed to follow recommendations, provide information, pay for services, and otherwise do as health professionals expect. A patient of record is an individual who has been treated under such terms and thus enjoys specific rights, such as access to continuing and emergency care, or access to their records.

The patients of one dentist are not automatically patients of another, and, in some cases, would not be accepted as patients. The ADA Code of Professional Conduct allows some latitude to practitioners in selecting their patients, although patient status cannot be determined by characteristics such as disability or sexual orientation. However, this must be determined by the dentist's competence to treat the presenting conditions.

The noun "patient" — a person who has agreed to the terms of treatment — and the adjective "patient" — minor suffering without complaint — have the same root. In that sense, the title of this column is essentially redundant.

Sociologist Talcott Parsons coined the phrase "sick role" to describe societal expectations around the notion of debilitating health. Those who are sick are excused from many obligations, such as going to school or work, and even excused from observing polite etiquette. It is a precondition of this status that they did not choose to be sick, as by excessive drinking, reckless driving, overeating, or refusing to brush one's teeth. A second condition on the sick role is that individuals must exercise personal responsibility for seeking competent help and following expert advice.

American society has changed since Parsons developed his ideas about the sick role more than half a century ago. We have, through the American with Disabilities Act and other legislation, relaxed the precondition about sickness not resulting from personal choice. The access issue is all about the second condition – personal responsibility and seeking help. Access is not a numbers issue (as the proportion of Americans receiving dental care is slightly better than in times past). The debate we are not having are over the conditions that must be fulfilled to qualify for care, with individuals seeming to abandon some of their responsibility for their own health and practitioners seeming to expect to concentrate their service on the most idealized cases. The conversation we are avoiding is about what it means to be a patient.

The nub:

1. Review the conditions individuals in need of oral health care must meet to qualify as patients in your practice.
2. We should ask ourselves how patient we are with our patients.
3. The patient issue is who has access to whom and under what conditions.

Ethical Resources

Matt Mullin

In a mining camp in the California Gold Country, a newcomer was questioning a veteran about two individuals he had seen arguing belligerently. When he passed by again, they were still locked in hostile exchange. The newcomer thought it ridiculous and gave his opinion that one of them should just shoot the other and have done with it. The old-timer slowly shook his head, "The first one to step out of the argument would be admitting he didn't have sufficient reason for his position."

Philosophers describe unsuccessful attempts to control others with their arguments as "lacking ethical resources." Simply put: Lacking resources means one's ethical position can't get the work done. Those whose ethical resources are inadequate may see where they want to go, but they can't get there, so they get mad. It is a very common situation.

The American philosopher Charles Stevenson developed a theory in the 1950s built on ethics as indignation. A sure sign that one had an ethical issue in hand would be how good it felt to use words like "reprehensible," "disgusted," "incredulous." Stevenson is no longer a force in ethics because his emotional theory lacks ethical resources. "I dislike commercialism in dentistry and you should too" only works well among those who already dislike commercialism. Good stuff for editorials, though.

High on the list of necessary resources for ethical positions are statements of best action and good reasons. Show them a better way, and most folks will respond, dentists often being among the first. And it is human nature that we prefer to have a reason in hand just in case we are questioned as we venture into new territory.

It is more resourceful to identify the best alternative than to gloat over failings. It also saves time: It is inefficient to get people to go where they should by telling them where not to go. And since all human action is imperfect, we will never get anywhere trying to cater to all those who have reservations.

Reasons are great resources, especially the general ones that cover many situations and can be subscribed to by a range of individuals. Reasons serve as places where people who disagree on some points can stand together to see if they have anything in common.

There is much in life that is annoying and just shouldn't be so. Getting mad is understandable, but not very helpful. Instead, get resourceful: articulate the best course forward and present your reasons. There are others who are doing the same.

The nub:

1. Use your emotional reaction to what you find unsettling in dentistry as a personal prompt to begin ethics work, not as a finished product you want to share.
2. Think through, with the help of others if possible, whether there are better (but not necessarily perfect) alternative actions; promote the best solution.
3. Give reasons for what you favor in dentistry: The more inclusive and general your reasons, the more powerful they will be.

Hippocratic Oath

Matt Mullin

In the 5th century B.C. Western world, the leading school was located on the island of Cos, just off the coast of what now is Turkey. Its "dean" is known to us as Hippocrates. About 1,000 pages of notes from the curriculum have been preserved in what now is called the Hippocratic Corpus. These describe the structure, functioning, and treatment of glands, fistulas, ulcers, etc. From this we can tell that the Hippocratic approach was medical, rather than surgical, with the goal being to preserve or restore the natural balance of the body. These old Greeks would have thought remineralization was just the thing.

There must have been a practice management course as well since we have short tracts on how the physician is to comport himself. Advice is given on how the professional should smell, how to "maintain a serious but not harsh countenance," and "looking as plump as nature intended him to be."

There is also a segment of about 250 words speaking directly to professionalism that we know today as the Hippocratic oath. It is chiefly known for a famous line about not causing harm that may well be the most frequently used title for editorials in the dental profession. More on that in a minute.

The oath specifically forbids three procedures: physician-assisted suicide, abortion, and surgery for gallstones. The latter is to be referred to specialists, something that we find in the American Dental Association Code of Professional Conduct, 2B. Confidentiality is strongly urged: see 1B in the ADA Code. The oath also prohibits "all mischief and in particular of sexual relations with both female and male persons, be they free or slaves." This one the ADA House decided not to take a position on a few years ago.

One element of the Hippocratic oath that dental educators have always envied is the ancient admonition that young physicians be treated as "the nephews" of practitioners, to be welcomed into the profession, and given financial support. Even more, those who take the oath agree to teach without fee. Only a few today honor that commitment through teaching in dental schools or speaking at scientific sessions without honoraria.

Now about that well-known line: "First, do no harm." It is not in the Hippocratic oath. "Premum non nicere" is Latin, and as nearly as anyone can work out, it is only several hundred years old. It is actually a fairly dim view of professionalism, sounding more like something a lawyer would say to protect the dentist rather than encouragement of public service. The phrase in the Hippocratic oath that is sometimes pointed out says "I will use my medications for the benefit of patients and not to harm them." Loose translation, "I will not poison anyone."

The nub:

1. The ethical foundation of the healing professions is ancient.
2. Volunteer to teach in a dental or dental hygiene school nearby or write a check to the CDA Foundation.
3. If you want to practice evidence-based dentistry, first, check your references.

Information Morality

Matt Mullin

It is surprising how many folks believe the "P" in HIPAA stands for "privacy." And the "I" in HIPAA must represent "information." So the law is assumed to protect patients' rights to privacy in health information. HIPAA actually stands for the Health Insurance Portability and Accountability Act, and there is a whole branch of philosophy concerned with information morality.

HIPAA has little to say about privacy, but Title 2 of the act — which is called, in true Washington style, the Administrative Simplification Section — goes on for pages about confidentiality and security.

Privacy is freedom from forced disclosure of personal information. The Fifth Amendment to the Constitution states that one cannot be compelled to offer self-incriminating information. Institutional review boards protect potential research subjects from revealing personal information, by answering questions or providing biometric data, if that is what they wish. Privacy concerns what is revealed or discoverable.

Confidentiality is a reasonable expectation that revealed information will not be passed along to others or used in unauthorized ways. It concerns what can be disclosed. Selling names on mailing lists, gossip about patients, and some would argue the National Provider Data Bank, are examples of breached confidentiality, not privacy.

Security is a matter of taking reasonable precaution to ensure against unintentional breaches of confidence. Information security includes coding patient information with protected keys, training for personnel, and rules and protocols that reduce the likelihood somebody else getting information for unwarranted use.

The morality of privacy is anything but clear. People pay psychiatrists to listen to their private matters. Companies spend fortunes to tell you what you should think of them. We readily cough up our Social Security and credit card information to buy goofy things on the Internet. Dentists are on sound moral grounds refusing care to patients who decline to provide health history information vital to treatment.

Consider this story. A woman and her daughter were enjoying a day at the beach until a group of teenagers established themselves nearby and engaged in extremely loud, personal conversation, and nearly completely disrobed. The mother complained to them that she could hear and see too much. The teenagers were indignant. "Mind your own business." The teenagers wanted to control both what information was revealed and what use could be made of it. So did the mother. The privacy concerns in this case are very complex.

The moral solution is that privacy needs to be negotiated, especially in health care. Immorality comes in failing to get necessary information and in breaking the negotiated agreement about how information is to be treated.

The nub:

1. Informed consent should include negotiation over the minimal amount of information both the patient and dentist will need for effective treatment.
2. Revealing information provided for the purpose of effective treatment for personal gratification, curiosity, or profit is abuse of power.
3. Protect the trust you have been given, even from accidental loss.

Ethics and Charity

Deborah Zemke

Americans are among the world's most generous people — professionals especially so. The ADA estimates that donated dentistry amounts to about 5 percent of the total oral health care. Dentists care and they give. But does that make them ethical? Perhaps we are mixing up ethics with charity.

Most dentists are aware of the distinction between what is legal and what is ethical. A few dentists might go to jail for systematically overbilling insurance companies, but who is incarcerated for overtreating patients? Professionalism is an agreement on behalf of patients but not an agreement with them.

But certainly, doing good for others is, per definition, ethical, right? Well, hiring your wife as a paid political consultant might not be (if it is nepotism). Giving a blood transfusion to a Christian Scientist is questionable. Withholding information about alternative treatments to steer patients toward optimal care is really questionable. Volunteering for a mission in Haiti is wonderful, but volunteering in the local nursing home might be more wonderful.

In the examples above, the person performing the good determines what the recipient should have, or even whether they should have anything at all. Both charity and paternalism add to the store of good in the world. But no one would be criticized for failing to provide them. It is a voluntary choice for the giver. But ethics is mandatory.

Imagine a dentist and a patient sitting across from each other engaged in a conversation about the optimal approach to treatment. There is a knowledge and skill dimension of this conversation and it is heavily weighted in favor of the professional. But simply knowing what can be done and how to do it does not make one ethical. There is almost always a situational advantage for the practitioner having to do with status, control of the environment, etc. But being in charge is hardly equivalent to being ethical. There are legal, professional, and other differences that favor the dentist, but none of these add up to ethics.

By process of subtraction, imagine that all of the circumstantial asymmetries between the dentist and the patient can be set aside. All that remains is a realization that the two people facing each other are fundamentally the same. They care about their futures; they want to know if there is a way of collaborating; they recognize that the person they are talking with is basically like them.

That is the basis of ethics. At that level, whatever you agree to will be ethical because it treats both parties the same, provided, of course, you are not colluding to bilk society.

The nub:

❶ Informed consent ensures that patients are given sufficient information to relate as ethical equals with oral health-care providers.

❷ Most of our dissatisfaction with technicians, officials, and insurance representatives stems from having to relate on their terms.

❸ Professionals find it easy to substitute charity for ethics: that allows them to retain their power over the situation.

The Genealogy of Ethics

Matt Mullin

We have put a man on the moon, manufactured Kevlar body armor, and destroyed several diseases to make way for others. But what has civilization done to change human nature? Philosophy sometimes gets a bad rap because there is almost no evidence that 2,500 years of talking about it has made us more ethical.

Part of the problem is that we have moved the target. Not raised the bar: just changed what it means to be ethical. Ethics has a genealogy.

The job of ethics, according to Socrates, is to decide how we are to live our lives. The powerful and wealthy of his day hired tutors to coach them so they would appear to be ethical in their civic roles. If Socrates were to drop in today, he would see that the ethical enterprise is being managed by Oprah Winfrey, Disney, and the Tea Party. It is no surprise that the preferred flavor of ethics in business schools today is called "virtue ethics," a revival of the old Greek ideal of looking good in public.

Actually, his program did not work out so well for Socrates, as a democratic government came to power in Athens in 399 BC and put him to death for corrupting the youth by teaching them to question. Aristotle did better because one of this pupils was the tyrant Alexander the Great.

The Dark Ages, medieval times, and especially the Renaissance redefined ethics as a matter of adherence to authority. Face it: the world was a scary and dangerous place. If folks did what they were told by powers temporal and ecclesiastical they might stand a chance. Ethics by authority carried over to the Inquisition.

The Enlightenment of the 18th century replaced authority with cooperation among reason-giving individuals, hence the American and French revolutions. But that created a new problem: How are we to decide what is really right and wrong if we have to listen to other people who are like us? The past 300 years has been an effort to ground ethics in either pure or peer reason, all the time allowing more and more people to participate in the discussion.

Many scholars feel that we are coming to the end of the Enlightenment. Too much self-interest has soiled the game. Efforts to "cap the oil spill of rampant individualism" by passing laws, redefining ethics as professional or corporate practice, or making it an academic discipline in the universities have not been satisfying.

I am still trying to work out how I should live my life, but whatever society decides is ethics for our time, we must recognize that our genecology involves fitting in with the power elite, recognizing authority, and giving reason to our peers.

The nub:

1. It is worth trying to answer the question "How should I live?"
2. Do not be surprised if others define ethics differently.
3. Do not let others define ethics for you: do not define it without involving others.

Dental Care Is Not a Right

Matt Mullin

The study of rights is a branch of ethics. But it is not mainstream, so the branch office is small. There is almost no one there working in the "Health as a Right" department.

Rights exist to the extent that someone declares they should have something and others agree. Sometimes the rights are positive, as in free public education, and sometimes they are negative, as in freedom from unwarranted search or seizure. Rights are claimed, they are not earned. Human rights belong to all people, without qualification. Civil rights belong to members of national groups, and that is why habeas corpus is a civil right in the United States but not in Iran. Entitlements are benefits or protections written into law for the advantage of specific groups, such as Medicaid, Indian gaming, or environmental protections.

Rights create obligations. Somebody must provide the resources that make positive rights possible and guarantee that negative rights are protected against encroachment. There are no free rights, they are always transfers from one segment of a group to another.

The United Nations' Declaration of Human Rights lays out rights such as fair remuneration for one's work, political assembly, and no slavery. Health is mentioned, but not as many people would imagine. Article 25 states that "Everyone has the right to a standard of living adequate for the health and well-being of himself and of his family." But that is different in nature from free public education: it is a test standard for economic development. It is not a right to health, but a right to choose health.

Leading philosophers today such as John Rawls and Norman Daniels state specifically that health is not a right. Jeremy Bentham, the late 18th century English jurist and philosopher, said, "Rights are utter nonsense, nonsense on stilts."

I count myself among those who boggle at the prospect of health care as a right. It is a bottomless opportunity to consume resources. There are more researchers developing health innovations than there are folks creating resources. America's health bill is now at 18 percent of the GDP and on its way up. And if an individual believes that somebody else owes them health care, who will say they have enough of it?

The alternative is to consider health, including oral health, as a social good. The public is damaged by children who miss school and employees who miss work because of toothache. Emergency rooms, by law, cannot turn patients with oral complications away despite this being an inefficient system. To the extent that the public chooses to avoid these social costs by subsidizing dentistry it should enact entitlements, but not more than that.

The nub:

❶ No one is entitled to everything they want just because they want it: try sharing your own list with others.

❷ When evaluating proposals for entitlements, ask whether the burdens as well as the benefits are being justly distributed.

❸ Try to answer the question for yourself: How much oral health care is enough?

The Duty to Punish

Matt Mullin

The teenager murdered her parents and then threw herself on the mercy of the courts because she was an orphan. Something is morally wrong with this picture. Any society that puts too much distance between breaking the rules and accepting the consequences will be a failure. Most people realize that, but we disagree on how to make it work.

We expect everyone to play by the rules in the game of life. If we know that the rules and penalties are only pretend, we will pretend to follow them just to keep the playing field level. Failure to enforce the rules of society is an ethical failing on society's part. Technically, society reneges on its promises to ensure the conditions for common moral behavior.

Good theory, but why is it so often honored in the breach?

Punishment has a cost that must be borne. Somebody should do something about this. It has always been fashionable for legislators to pass laws to demonstrate their moral concern and then underfund enforcement. "People should just do what is right" is the wimpiest of false ethics imaginable. "I talked to them about it" does not get much work done either.

The fact that we get as much morality as we can afford is a doubly difficult problem. The benefit of ethical behavior is to society generally, the cost is to specific individuals or groups. We often seek to pass the cost of punishment onto others. The hangman of old wore a mask and was excluded from society.

Individuals can actually filch personal prestige by short-circuiting punishment. In every culture, granting clemency is a sign of high social status. Only the governor can commute the death sentence. When we say "I am letting it go this time," we elevate our own status. In surveys of cheating in colleagues, the most common response to detected cheating is for faculty members to "deal with the problem on a personal and individual basis."

In addition to wanting to be judge and jury by personally dispensing mercy, we like to be legislators as well. When we selectively wink at punishment, we are changing the rules. It is perfectly appropriate in a democracy to work to change the rules, say the laws requiring reporting of suspected child abuse. It is not appropriate to ignore the rules and expect to be exempt for the consequences.

Finally, society is lousy at matching punishment to unwanted behavior. Extreme forms of punishment have no more effect on behavior than do barely effective ones. One of my favorite cartoons shows the hangman placing a noose on the criminal's head and saying, "I hope this teaches you a lesson." On the other side, penalties that society is not willing to enforce are useless.

The nub:

1. In ethics, don't expect to get anything you are not willing to pay for.
2. Don't expect to control other's ethical behavior by paying the costs with others' resources.
3. Beware private justice.

Confabulation

I have been confabulating a little more recently than I like. I did some over the weekend and felt embarrassed, though it seemed innocent enough at the time.

Confabulation baristas blend mostly truth and a little bit of creative self-deception. Its function is to make us look better than we really are. It is all about us. And it is quite natural, unless it gets carried away into narcissism.

Every time a successful full-mouth reconstruction is recounted, the initial patient condition becomes more challenging. At the peer-review hearing, the patient was "belligerently noncooperative" rather than slow in payments. It is reported that the number of people who say they were at the SF Giants and Oakland A's World Series game when the Loma Prieta earthquake hit in 1989 is four to five times the capacity of the Candlestick Park.

Matt Mullin

Confabulation really is an ethical issue. We should not be saying things just because we want them to be true. Confabulations are small in order to be believable. But a lot of small distortions, a habit of shaving the truth, may undermine public trust more than a whopper one has to back away from by claiming hyperbole or puffery.

Sir Frederick Bartlett was a British psychologist who studied memory in the 1920s and 1930s. He is the fellow who invented the "telephone game" where A gets a message to pass on to B who repeats it to C, etc. The message becomes hopelessly garbled by the time it gets to the end of the chain despite all communicator thinking they have been faithful. More than a knock on human foibles, Bartlett proved two things: First, memories are not permanent neural configurations like letters in a filing cabinet. They are dynamic and they change over time. Second, these changes are not random. Memory drifts toward stereotypes or ideals. When we confabulate, our recollections tend toward idealized representations of ourselves.

In one of Bartlett's most famous experiments, he showed subjects an ambiguous outline drawing of an elongated extension with uneven knobs at each end. Sometimes the picture was labeled "barbell"; sometimes it was labeled "drumstick." When individuals were asked sometime later to draw the picture from memory, those who saw the picture labeled barbell exaggerated the symmetry of the knobs, and the more times they drew the picture from memory, the more idealized the barbell became. The same happened for the drumstick, but this time the image converged on an idealized chicken leg. No verbal confusion was involved: he considered only drawings.

Our memory is a flatterer. It is just a little dishonest to confabulate: It is just a little dangerous for us to believe our own confabulations. Nub:

1. When we report on our accomplishments, we are revealing to ourselves what kind of person we think we want to be.
2. Be careful: someone may call our bluff.
3. It is unethical to ask others to believe in a world that we know is a slight exaggeration.

A lot of small distortions, a habit of shaving the truth, may undermine public trust more than a whopper one has to back away from by claiming hyperbole or puffery.

Practical Morality

Matt Mullin

Confucius said (really, he did): A country will experience eternal prosperity if the ruler can govern ethically for a single day. We're still waiting.

All of us make the effort from time to time, but we are morally flawed. One of the common flaws is to talk as though perfection were something worth talking about. I propose that we stop talking about perfection because that gives us an excuse for stopping when we feel like it. Instead we should focus on achieving a practical level of moral behavior.

Most immoral behavior is committed by people who consider themselves to be basically ethical. Several years ago it was reported by the California State Attorney General that insurance companies had overcharged drivers by $5.2 billion. Later the media reported that during the same period, drivers had submitted an estimated $6 billion in fraudulent claims.

Is there an acceptable level of corruption? Of course there is, and we are all experts at detecting it. I would be happy to hear refutations of this claim from anyone who has never once driven over the speed limit, told a lie, or encouraged a patient to undergo a procedure they did not really need.

Fortunately there is a definable level of practical morality between ethical anarchy and abstract ethical perfection. In fact, the Nobel laureate John Nash, about whom the movie *A Beautiful Mind* was made, proved that there is such a practical but not perfect level in every situation. This can be defined very precisely in mathematical terms if one wants to take the trouble. But most often we sense intuitively what a society will accept in terms of minor indiscretions and when we have crossed the line. We are creatures of practical moral common sense. In technical terms, this optimal practical fair point in human relations is called the "equilibrium": a point where each of us can expect nothing better from everyone, including ourselves.

Editorials, sermons, things we tell our children, and hypocrisy are all about perfection. There are two reasons why there is always a gap between perfection and the general moral behavior in a community. First, there has never been agreement about how to define moral perfection. Second, perfection is not humanly sustainable.

This is not a discussion about moral relativism. Anyone who cheats in the game of life, anyone who attempts to get more than his or her fair share at the expense of others by distorting the rules of the communities should be punished. They are immoral. Anyone who tries to live in that zone between the value of the game and perfection has my complete admiration. But I don't expect to be lectured to by them.

The nub:

1. Don't mistake preaching about perfection for being moral in a practical sense.
2. Always prefer accepting the flawed nature of others to hypocrisy.
3. Judge the adequacy of moral behavior by this rule: Have I made all the improvements in the world that were available to me?

Billy Budd

Omniscience means knowing everything. Naturally, it would come in handy in the "Whose smartest at the table" kinds of competitions. But it is generally recognized that the number of truly omniscient individuals is very small and phony know-it-alls are real pains.

Surprisingly, we are slower at recognizing that the same sort of limitations apply in the ethical domain. If a genie offered me the gift of knowing what everybody else should do, I would be sorely tempted to turn it down.

Consider the case of *Billy Budd, Sailor.* This is the title of Herman Melville's posthumously published novella, now a standard text in high school. Budd is a merchant sailor pressed into the British Navy (kidnapped at sea) in 1797. Described as "beautiful Billy," Melville makes him a Christ-like paragon of virtue: an able seaman, loyal, popular, and even gifted as a peacemaker. His only flaws include a touch of righteous indignation and stammering under emotional pressure. Never in the novella is there even a hint the reader learns of that Budd is anything less than pure virtue. The fact that he is hanged, and even Budd praises the captain who orders it, makes for a nice ethical discussion.

The plot unfolds like this: John Claggart, the master-at-arms (shipboard chief of police), is jealous of Billy Budd and fabricates circumstantial evidence of his being involved in a mutiny plot. Claggart reports Budd to Capt. Vere and the captain calls in Budd to confront his false accuser. In complete disbelief and unable to express himself otherwise, Budd lashes out at Claggart and lands a single, fatal blow.

The moral challenge is what should Capt. Vere do? Budd is guilty of three breaches of the British Articles of War: failure to report the attempts by Claggart to frame him, making a threat to a superior officer, and committing murder. Striking a superior officer (regardless of the effect) normally called for summary execution. There are no doubts about the facts. Vere saw it with his own eyes.

Melville really piles it on Vere. He and Budd were the only witnesses. Budd's ship, with the absolutely inappropriate name Bellipotent, had pursued a French warship and become separated from the fleet so that Vere could not appeal to others. The story is set a few years following the well-publicized mutiny on the ship Bounty and several notorious navy uprisings in English ports, creating a climate hypersensitive to organized insubordination.

In his heart, Vere "knows" Budd was set up. He convenes a drum head court of his officers. They hear the testimony and condemn Budd to be hanged the next morning. Just before Budd is raised on a yard arm with a rope around his neck to suffocate, he cried out "God bless Captain Vere."

Modern readers regard Vere's verdict as wrong-headed, harsh, insensitive, the triumph of a callous system over the virtuous individual, or simple cruelty. They regard Budd's opinion on the matter as mockery or irony.

Such a judgment can only be justified based on omniscience. The reader is sucked into a position of false moral superiority by being given a view of the situation that no one in the novella actually had. That is a common ethical trap. We like easy answers, and are tempted to make up facts that justify the outcome we prefer. Knowing only what Vere knew or what the officers who sat at the court martial knew, there is no other judgment that could be reached. Budd is truly prescient in praising Vere: He saw that Vere did what he had to do and that armchair second-guessers would not even have been allowed to give testimony. Melville has pulled a dirty trick on the reader by making him or her seem morally superior by taking a position that no one could actually take.

In years of leading students and practicing dentists through ethics cases involving second opinions and justifiable criticism of colleagues, I am struck by the assumptions that are added to the case by participants. The best way to get out of a dilemma is to assume some additional facts that justify our conclusion: "The patient may just be shopping for a lower price," or "Perhaps this is the kind of patient who is mad at the world in general."

Matt Mullin

Psychologists such as Nobel laureate Daniel Kahneman and Amos Tversky have studied what people make up in order to make sense of ambiguous situations. A common scenario used in their research is a college professor driving home and diverting his normal route to run an errand for his wife. He is struck by a truck and dies. Virtually, no one is willing to leave the story as told, accepting the facts as random events. Human nature requires that we invent "if onlys" in order to make the story meaningful to us. Here are some of the common characteristics of makeup explanations: Bad things require explanatory stories; there is something that needs fixing in the world if things do not turn out as we would like. Good outcomes are accepted as one's due. The explanations are simple, single changes in the world — the brakes failed — not the truck took the wrong turn, and the professor started late, and the brakes failed. The best fix is that the other guy should have acted otherwise.

The nub:

1. There is no view from nowhere. It is unethical to presume ethical omniscience.
2. Moral courage means deciding based on everything that is known, not what is imagined.
3. Be humble about what you do not know.

Muda Ethics

Matt Mullin

"Muda" is a Japanese word for an activity that is wasteful or unproductive. The West became familiar with it through the quality movement. Here is how the concept of "muda" relates to ethics in oral health care:

Reduced waste promotes quality, which leads to reduced cost. Because health care is a limited resource, reducing cost means that more people can have better oral health. It is unethical to raise costs unnecessarily or to avoid taking reasonable steps to reduce cost. At least that is what most of us think about cable TV monopolies, insurance companies, and government services.

Waste is any activity that does not add value. Would patients pay to sit in the waiting room? Would they pay for a full-mouth X-ray series having just had one before moving to a new town? Would they pay for fixing joint pain from a crown that was too high? Would dentists pay themselves what they pay a hygienist or assistant when doing work that can be delegated?

The muda concept begins by envisioning an office that runs smoothly, giving every patient exactly what is required the first time in the most efficient manner possible. Everything that falls short of that ideal is waste; it adds to cost without contributing value. Some offices work continuously to reduce waste; others are content to accept some level of waste. A few team members even celebrate their skill at fixing problems and would dread the prospect of losing that opportunity. This is muda by design. And anybody who sees an opportunity to increase their personal influence or profit from inefficiency will be a closet critic of quality.

The experts tell us there are eight categories of waste. Defects are an obvious example. Somebody has to pay for redos or for work that is not as serviceable as what could have been done instead. Overproduction is a second type. In the dental office, this includes overtreatment and performing work before it is needed. Moving things around unnecessarily and waiting are also examples of waste. Patient scheduling inefficiencies is the obvious example, but staff members can also be affected. Reducing unproductive motion is one area where dentistry has driven down muda. But overprocessing, doing work to standards above what is required, is a type of waste that professionals tend to embrace. It is understandable that experts will want to use all of their talent, but it is uncertain that treating one patient to the acme of care is better than treating two to a professionally acceptable level. The squandering of talent is a final kind of waste.

The Nub:

1. Ethics is a pattern, not an event. We are judged by the overall impact of our lives, not specific acts that we select for evaluation.
2. Oral health care resources are limited: it is unethical to waste them.
3. It is better to design systems that minimize waste than to become famous for fixing symptoms.

The Five Cs

Matt Mullin

Every individual who seeks dental care should expect it to be comprehensive, continuous, competent, compassionate, and coordinated.

Comprehensive oral care means treating the whole patient. Emergency care, the first tentative restorative work, and recall appointments should all be performed with a view toward the best overall level of health achievable. Treating up to the allowable insurance coverage or prioritizing options based on the best margin for the dentist are simply unethical. Placing cosmetic concerns first, even when the patient requests it, is a moral minefield.

Continuous care aims for a lifetime of oral health. Arguably the greatest cause of suboptimal oral health is episodic treatment. Patients who go to the dentist only when it hurts have missed the ideal time for intervention (during the early stages of disease or before) and often accept only that treatment needed to remove the symptoms. Except for trauma, virtually all oral problems are chronic conditions. The fact that dentistry and medicine are compensated "per intervention" and that late interventions often return the largest profits, creates an ethical challenge. There is no CDT code for creating the habit of continuous care, but dentists who practice as if there were are the paragons of professionalism.

Competent care meets or exceeds professional standards. Patients expect the level of care the profession as a whole promotes to the public. Every intervention may not be flawless. There are legitimate surprises and unanticipated circumstances. What counts against an ethic of competence is the dentist not having a justifiably high expectation of a satisfactory outcome going into the treatment. This also covers dentists not knowing whether they are competent or not. A general dentist who botches a molar endo is incompetent on three grounds: endodontic technique, diagnosis, and ethical standards.

Compassionate dental care is considerate of the entire patient, including his or her values. Pressuring or tricking a patient into accepting a treatment option that the dentist feels is optimal but which the patient would regret if fully informed is questionably ethical. There are emotional, economic, status, self-image, and family dimensions of oral health. Care that is otherwise excellent but fails to address these concerns may meet the dentist's but not the patient's needs. It is presumptuous.

Coordinated care recognizes that oral health is provided by a collective resource, and patients should have the benefit of the full team. This includes hygienists, patient education and financial counseling staff members, specialists, and colleagues who are available for consultation. Communication among members of the larger oral health care team and with the patient are the keys to coordinated care.

The Nub:

1. The best evidence of a dentist's skill is not a before-and-after photo: it is the patient's history in the charts.
2. Dentists judge the success of their careers over a lifetime, using a range of criteria: the same standard applies to successful patient care.
3. Patients cannot be forced to participate across the five Cs of care, but they should always be given the opportunity.

The Practical Ethics Syllogism

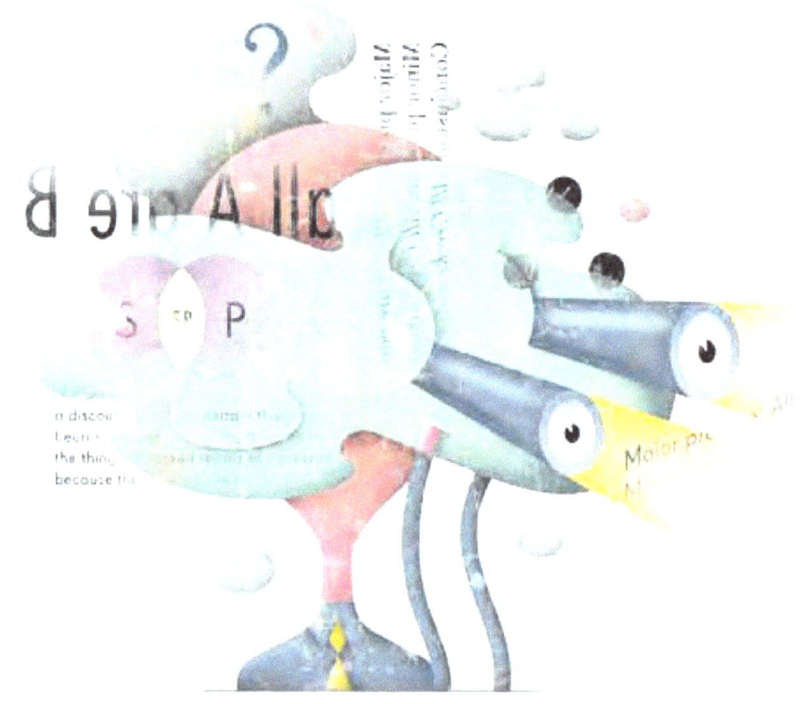
Matt Mullin

It is an ethical absolute, enshrined in the Ten Commandments: Thou shalt not kill. There is something reassuring in such great rules. "Always put the patients' interests first" and "First, do no harm." Folks will surely recognize us as ethical if we claim we don't lie, we refrain from coercing others, and we do unto others as we would be done by.

The problem is that this level of ethics is in the clouds; when we bring it down to where we normally live, things become more nuanced. Moses found this out. Very shortly following the part about "Thou shalt not kill" being carved in stone we find "For every one that curseth his father and his mother shall be surely put to death (Leviticus 20:9) and a little farther on in Ecclesiastes, "To everything there is a season ... A time to kill and a time to heal." Most people would go along with killing in self-defense. They would also coerce a child from running into traffic and draw some sort of a line around putting the patients' interests first if that involves unhealthy practices or free treatment.

This tension between the abstract and the practical is known as the practical ethics syllogism.

In situations where Rule X is applicable, do A.

This is a situation where Rule X is appropriate.

Therefore do A.

When finished treatment by specialist, return patient to GP.

This patient may or may not need specialty care.

Therefore?

Cases of suspected child abuse must be reported by health professions.

It is hard to tell exactly what caused these bruises.

Therefore?

The ethical principle is always honored as true without exception. But the practical application of the principle is open to interpretation. In our court system, judges state the law but juries determine its applicability in specific cases.

Here is how some philosophers approach the problem. Interpretation is where the action is, and it is dependent on context and group membership. What it means to be a responsible adult is to have internalized the interpretative norms of the community. When a colleague is ready for a position in organized dentistry, you will know by the way he or she sees the issues. I offer no apologies for faculty members who would deny a degree to a student who is a technical wizard but does not embody the values of the profession.

Becoming a moral dentist is mostly about being able to spot problems and interpret them the way one's colleagues do. That is why most dental school courses in ethics now teach using cases.

The Nub:

1. It is more important to read your colleagues than to read books about ethics.
2. Too little consensus in a profession about how to interpret situations is bad; so is too much.
3. The hall talk about claims made in C.E. courses is more important than the before and after slides.

Moral Decoupling

All the big companies have ethics departments now. Recently failing to find a contact on the webpage of the first large dental supplier I tried, I left a note on the bulletin board explaining who I am and asking to be put in touch. A few days later, I received a reply that "Yes, X Company does have an ethics officer, a lawyer, and, in fact, a whole ethics staff, but corporate policy prevents releasing any information about them."

Welcome to "decoupling" — the practice of separating the form of ethical compliance from its substance. Some examples include requiring that employees receive "ethics training"; issuing reports and codes of conduct; filing compliance reports; conflict of interest disclosure for publications and presentations; whistle-blowing legislation; and good PR. A conspicuous example of ethical form over substance is the Sarbanes-Oxley laws enacted after the Enron scandal and requiring that higher-ups in organizations file papers saying they know what is going on in the firm. Not much teeth in that gesture from our legislative master decouplers. This has been a boost toward full employment for lawyers, but there is absolutely no evidence in almost 10 years that the trajectory of corporate opportunism in America has been bent.

Research in the field shows that ethical rules for organizations have these effects: increased formal appearance, increased cost, and increased employee and public cynicism. Ethical behavior is a function of the way leaders in the firm act, especially how they respond when challenged, not what they say.

Decoupling has become established in our legal system. The U.S. Sentencing Commission Organizational Guidelines (accessible on the Web) prescribe the formulas used in sanctioning businesses that break the law. (I believe the guidelines apply only to organizations with 10 or more employees.) The guidelines are used to calculate a "culpability score" that drives the size of the fine. All organizations start with a base score of five points against the organization, and have points added or subtracted based on circumstances.

The base culpability score can double for large firms. Previous bad faith or criminal activity increase the penalty. If there has been an adjudication for similar misconduct during the past 10 years, add one point; if the firm violates a standing judicial order or injunction add either one or two points.

On the other hand, if the organization has an ethics compliance program, subtract three points. Firms with repeat violations of court injunctions can have that penalty removed by showing that they had an ethics compliance program — even when per definition that program failed. If the firm cooperates in the investigation, it gets another two-point bonus. That comes pretty close to letting the form of ethics compliance erase the negative effect of violating the intent of ethical (legal) guidelines.

Ethical behavior is a function of the way leaders in the firm act, especially how they respond when challenged, not what they say.

The Nub:

1. Decoupling form from substance in ethics does not promote moral excellence.
2. Decoupling form from substance in ethics promotes cynicism.
3. Codes, pronouncements, and training are insufficient evidence of commitment to a moral culture.

Rule of Double Causes

The connection between what we do and the reasons we give for doing it are sloppy. As William Jennings Bryan observed, "It is a sorry mind that can't think up some reason for what we want to do." The big problem is that there is no one-to-one correspondence between actions and justifications. Most actions go without justification. They just do not need to be explained. But there are some actions that have multiple explanations. That is where the concern for the Rule of Double Cause comes in.

You make a donation to a charitable cause in the name of a revered colleague. You feel good about it until you see in the publication of the organization you supported that the list of donors omitted your name and your contribution, which would have been regarded by all who saw it as generous. Should you say something? This situation uncovers a "double cause." Was the contribution made out of respect for your colleague and the cause or out of a desire for personal recognition? If both motives were involved, what is the relative weight of each, and was the charitable motive strong enough to have carried the day by itself?

A dentist has just invested thousands of dollars on courses and equipment to add a new service line to the practice. The dentist has been advised by their advocates that a move to state-of-the-art procedures will boost a dentist's earnings from the 30th to the 70th percentile compared with dentists who only provide services that patients are most in need of. A patient presents who may very well be a good candidate for the new service. There is no doubt that, if performed successfully, the procedure would be beneficial. There is also no doubt that the dentist would gain financially and in terms of professional self-fulfillment. This is a case where the Rule of Double Cause applies.

Both motives (service and self-fulfillment) are part of the decision about the new procedure. In order to minimize the threat of self-dealing, the dentist should (a) honestly acknowledge all motives and engage the patient in a fully-informed decision, (b) make certain that the competence level in this never-before-attempted technique is high enough that success is assured, and (c) be prepared to stand by the outcomes of the procedure – including diminished service to traditional patients.

It may not be obvious, but the rules for untangling double causes are all about actions one takes and not about what one says. No one can argue his or her way to a moral position.

The Nub:

❶ Consider all the consequences of your choices, not just enough of them to justify what you want to do.

❷ Double causes can be untangled by imagining how one would respond if things did not work out as planned.

❸ It is inherently unethical to claim that one is acting only out of the most laudable of the multiple causes for a choice.

Truth Decay

Truth decay is a chronic, communicable disease and very common these days. It isn't exactly lying: It is just making sure that other's expectations are as favorable to our own interests as we can possible get away with. The epitome is the consent decree. Companies that have broken the law agree to pay a fee, without admitting any wrongdoing, in order that their conduct not be held against them or admitted into evidence in the future. It is like purchasing reputation insurance after the fact. The cost of such coverage in America seems to be declining.

Surprising to many, "Thou shalt not lie" is not one of the Ten Commandments. There is a biblical prohibition against perjuring oneself in a trial, but deceiving one's enemies is good strategy and misrepresenting the value of goods is sound business. American tourists are told, "It is your fault that your pockets were picked." Tragically, this caveat emptor attitude lingers with regard to rape, racism, and welfare. A close cousin of truth decay is paternalism. In a world where "father knows best," it is good to be the father.

When I was an experimental psychology major in college, we made a galvanic skin response version of a lie detector device. It worked well, except for one guy who always managed to defeat it. His strategy: for any question, he always added something: "Have you ever been unfaithful to a girlfriend?" became "Have you ever been unfaithful to a girlfriend names Ester?" I am afraid that is what Congressman Weiner did recently when he denied posting explicit photos, or professional athletes accused of doping, or dentists with misleading advertising claims or supersized treatment plans.

Veracity is not one of the four cardinal principles of bioethics. It was added by the American Dental Association, primarily to cover relationships among professionals, and it is by far the longest section of the Code of Professional Conduct. The code is specific in interdicting the following: "Dentists shall not represent the care (fees or advertisements) being rendered to their patients in a false or misleading manner"; "A dentist who recommends and performs unnecessary dental services or procedures is engaged in unethical conduct"; "The dentist has an independent obligation to inquire into the truth and accuracy of (manufacturers') claims and verify that they are founded on accepted scientific knowledge and research." "It is unethical for a dentist to increase a fee to a patient because the patient is covered under a dental benefits plan" and "The use of fellowships in advertising to the general public may be misleading."

The truth of our words and actions does not depend on logic; we must look to whether others can live by our words.

The nub:

❶ Truth has soft edges. Aim for the center, not the boundaries

❷ Avoiding lies is not the same thing as telling the truth.

❸ The truth is what others need to know to move forward with their lives.

Moral Bleaching

"Out, damn spot! Out, I say." Lady Macbeth, mentally deranged by the final act of William Shakespeare's play *The Tragedy of Macbeth*, cannot scrub her hands clean of the imagined blood of King Duncan, whom she and her husband have offed. What she needs is moral bleach.

The term — or its equivalent, ethical fading — has a technical meaning in philosophy. It refers to moving a moral violation sideways into the legal context and then buying one's way out. Consent decrees are a classical example. Businesses that engage in morally repugnant practices agree to settlements for monetary compensation without admitting guilt. That accomplishes two objectives: The costs of litigation are reduced; and, in most cases, the record of the past action is expunged and may not be used as evidence in future trials. But the great payoff is that one's conscience is wiped clean. The spot has been bleached away.

Before the onset of the age of instant social media communication, families with good names to protect bought off the dalliances of their scions (and probably still try). A speeding ticket can be fixed. A dentist can settle a disagreement with a patient. This is private justice — an accommodation between the concerned parties that does not involve society at large.

The best known research study on phenomenon of moral bleach involved problems day care centers have with parents picking up their children late. Reminders, admonitions, and appeals to responsibility did not work. Eventually, a group of day care centers hit upon the idea of charging a per-minute late fee to the foot-dragging patents. Big impact!

The rate and extent of delinquency increased dramatically under the new system. Parents figured that they were no longer responsible for their promises because they were purchasing the right to flout the rules. They had bleached their moral obligations. When the day care centers reverted to previous rules, the tardiness rate remained high. They had taught parents how to sidestep moral responsibility.

There is strong evidence in the psychology literature that extrinsic rewards push aside intrinsic ones.

About 30 years ago, I tested this idea in a dental school course. Students made health presentations at grade schools and submitted reports. All students received the same level of detailed objective feedback. Half of the reports were graded A through F (and the full range was evident), and half were simply told that their participation was sufficient. Students were later asked whether they had an interest in participating in such programs in the future and whether they intended to do this sort of thing as part of their practices. Results: Those who received an extrinsic reward in the form of a grade expressed significantly less interest in participating in this sort of public professional service. The grade bleached out a positive public attitude.

The Nub:

❶ We have been given a conscience for a reason: It is unwise to pay to disable it.

❷ Legal remedies are sometimes necessary, but they do not address moral failings.

❸ Is the modern epidemic of giving prizes for the sake of sponsor PR actually eroding the very motivation it claims to honor?

Low-cost Ethics

Most people favor ethics, lots of it. But they do not want to pay more for it than is necessary.

Charles Graeber's book *The Good Nurse : A True Story of Medicine, Madness and Murder,* tells the story of Charles Cullen, an effective nurse who worked at nine hospitals in New Jersey and Pennsylvania, and received sound employee ratings and letters of reference. He also murdered at least 40 patients.

Cullen was eventually brought to justice, and is now in prison, by the detective work of a police officer investigating a predatory assault incident outside the hospital, by a curious pharmacist and by a floor nurse. Authorities at some of the hospitals where Cullen worked had recognized the pattern and assembled the evidence — but none acted. He was forced to resign from five, but given neutral references. In his final position, the hospital was confronted by state authorities with the proof, but they deliberated for three months over concerns about the reputation to the hospital, financial implications and the possibility of lawsuits. During that time, Cullen killed five patients. When the authorities notified the hospital that they intended to arrest Cullen, the hospital fired him — because of irregularities on his employment application. The hospital obstructed the investigation, even lying about what evidence it had.

The hospitals certainly knew right from wrong. They just did not feel they could afford to be very ethical.

A story closer to home. In the 1980s, the University of the Pacific, Arthur A. Dugoni School of Dentistry adopted a standard for academic status based on contracts. Students who were not on track to become good dentists could be dismissed for either of two reasons: they participated in the contract, but it did not correct the deficiencies, or they declined to participate.

One morning I found myself facing a student in my office as academic dean and I heard these words: "You may think you are pretty clever demanding that I get psychiatric help. But you are wrong. You wait right here because I am going to housing to get a gun and when I come back, you'll see."

The student was brilliant — 4.0+ GPA from a top school — and his technical skills were fine. But the faculty had signaled that his relations with others were unstable and that he likely could not function as an independent professional. His family did phone and ask that I have him arrested (before the gun comment) "so he could get help." When I said that was their responsibility, they hung up on me. Other schools use an "objective" standard based on grades in order to protect their reputations and are often in court defending these actions. Pacific has not had a single lawsuit over dismissals since the system was put in place.

The nub:

1. You get what you pay for in ethics.
2. Sometimes others pick up the tab for the ethics we fancy — sometimes the cost to others can be extreme.
3. There must be evidence that one cares for the ethics one espouses.

Dancing With the Devil

In the little town of Sonoma where I live the north-south streets have numbers and those running east-west are named for countries such as Peru, Brazil and France. We used to have a Germany Street and an Italy Street, but during the Second World War, these became MacArthur and Patton. We don't dance with the devil.

The official policy of the United States is that we do not negotiate with terrorist devils and politicians must be free of conflicts of interest commercial devils. Dentists tend to see insurance companies and CE speakers sponsored by industry in this light.

Of course we dance with devils daily, and we complain loudly when others are dancing with more attractive ones. The government gives financial and arms support to dictators. Forty-five percent of dental care is underwritten by insurance. A few years ago the ADA signed a joint marketing agreement with Wrigley and the American Academy of Pediatric Dentistry accepted $1M from Coca-Cola. We have lobbyists in Sacramento and Washington.

There are two moral issues here: when should we dance with the devil and are we being hypocritical when we belly ache about the practice?

Every action has multiple motives. Whistle-blowers are entitled to handsome compensation under federal law. An ad in this journal may simultaneously turn a profit for the manufacturer and the dentist who uses it, as well as benefitting countless patients. We have to consider the whole set of pro and con reasons when deciding which devils to put on our dance card.

Here is where the conflict comes in. Dr. X sees the values associated with the ADA-Wrigley deal as reducing member dues, facilitating innovative programs, tarnishing the image of the profession and developing useful ties with industry – in that order. Dr. Y counts exactly the same benefits and liabilities, but with reputation of the profession as highest on the list. These dentists will disagree on the ADA's action and they probably will argue past each other, one saying it is a financial issue and the other saying it is a matter of professional integrity. Of course it is! Such conflicts are even internal. I have heard that at least one individual involved in the ADA-Wrigley deal has changed his mind. The priority of values depends on where we stand and when we look. Changing our value priorities after the fact is called moral regret.

Devil dancing is a rich opportunity for hypocrisy. Such double-steps usually take the form of emphasizing only the socially positive items on our own list of reasons and only the negative ones on others' lists. There is also hypocrisy of the loyal opposition. Those who do not receive a benefit from ADA's commercial activities because they are not members will be prompt in criticism of bent principles.

The Nub:

❶ Few choices in life are completely determined by a single principle.

❷ Different people choose different devils.

❸ Envy may cause us to criticize others' choices of devils.

Must Others Play By My Rules?

Aesop has the fable of the farmer and the snake, and there is a parallel tale of a turtle or frog and the scorpion or snake. The basic idea is that the farmer, turtle or frog gets a bite after being assured that there will be no bad outcomes from cooperation.

Recidivism is rampant. The patient most likely to no-show or skip on payments is the one who has done so before. he alcoholic is often a skillful and incorrigible liar, and those forced into a corner are usually dangerous. The medieval canon lawyer Grotius argued that it is ethical that those in great need steal because that is "natural."

Something does not seem quite right about this picture, however. Doesn't being moral mean exactly doing what is right, rising to a higher nature, especially when one has given one's word? Perhaps not.

Consider the case of lying. Odysseus was hugely admired in the Hellenistic world, especially because he told clever lies. Jacob cheated his father-in-law out of more than half his flock of sheep and the story is told approvingly in the book of Genesis. Virtually all cultures have a double standard regarding misleading those who are one's buddies and those in the out group.

There is much more at stake here than hair-splitting about how many fibs can dance on the head of a pin. It would be very convenient if everyone always did what he or she promised. Since we don't, our reflex response is to condemn the deceivers as unethical and leave it at that. They are not playing by the rules we wish to impose on them. If we can't have things our own way, at least we can be judgmental.

The alternative is to deal with our own circumstances and dreams and those of others on an equal and realistic footing. This requires a higher level of interpersonal empathy and greater moral skill, and it leads to a more flourishing sense of community than does the naïve approach of expecting that others will follow our personal ethical standards.

The wonderful thing about acting on an understanding of our own and others' interests and capabilities is that the joint best solution is self-enforcing. We do not need an outside authority to punish snakes that bite despite promising not to when we give them an appropriately wide berth. Gangs will not stop violence because it is against the law and the poor will not come to the dentist because we value good oral health. In every case, we must change the conditions on the ground rather than our opinions about them.

As the Scottish philosopher David Hume observed: "Nature is too strong for principle."

The nub:

1. Expect people to do what it is their nature to do, including oneself.
2. Understand others before imposing personal standards of right or wrong on them.
3. Change behavior by altering the way natural interests are expressed rather than through judgment.

The Illusion of an Objective Difference of Opinion

It is well known that if all the dental school deans are assembled in a room and asked to indicate whether their schools are in the top quartile, more than 25 percent of the hands will go up. It is a great relief that no schools are in the bottom quartile. But it begins to get a bit uncomfortable when study after study reports, as in fact they have, that well more than 50 percent of Americans are better than the median in terms of communication skills, empathy, sensitivity to others and ethics.

There is a double blindness working here. On average, we are wrong about how good we are at knowing whether we are right. Certainly a lot of other people are. I will present a brief list of features of our illusions of objectivity drawn from the three-volume collection of research papers edited by Nobel laureate in economics, Daniel Kahneman.

The most common form of this myopathy is called false consensus. We overestimate how many others see the world the same way we do. Asked what proportion of people approve or disapprove of capital punishment, we strongly fantasize that we are in the majority. Dentists overestimate the proportion of Americans who value oral health. We exaggerate the degree to which our personal ethical standards are shared. This naturally causes us to think of others as uninformed, mean spirited, self-interested or sneaky — or some of each — when there are disagreements.

In a famous study, fans from Dartmouth and Princeton watched a film of a close football game and recorded the number of "bad calls" by refs. Princeton fans saw the game as biased in Dartmouth's favor; and Dartmouth fans were certain it was the other way. Everybody knows that the media in America are biased; we just can't agree on which way they lean. Beware of volunteering as a neutral mediator as neutrality, like truth, is among the first casualties in disagreements.

We overrate the gaps that separate ourselves from others. We focus on the differences, and we tend to attribute the disparities to character traits of others (they are unreasonable) rather than to situational differences (they are coming at this with a different set of needs). Compromise is frightening, and we tend to avoid it by moving the goal posts if necessary.

People who share a conversation each think they have learned more about the other, even when they did most of the talking. We are quicker to spot potential bias in others' information set than in our own and more likely to rate others as being susceptible to propaganda than we are. We even think our own group is more subject to unfair stereotyping than others.

The nub:

1. It is human nature to be a little biased about how biased we are.
2. There is suspicion of those who claim to be neutral or entirely justified by evidence.
3. It is difficult to defend ethical positions as being objectively obvious.

Disclosure

The joke 150 years ago was that God never let the sun set on the British Empire because he didn't trust the Brits with the lights out. That is a version of the ethical chestnut "Don't do anything you would find awkward to have to explain."

This is a catchy ethical standard; good stuff for editorials. It is standard form to disclose conflicts of interest for C.E. speakers and authors of journal articles plumping new products and procedures. The FDA requires full warnings for therapeutic claims (but not for cosmetic ones). If Enron had only been transparent in reporting its financial dealings, American business would not be plagued with Sarbanes-Oxley reporting regulations. Sunshine is a good disinfectant. Disclosure is better. But neither should be used universally.

There are two problems with the "Don't do it if you wouldn't feel free to talk about it in public" rule. First, there is that little word "if." Moral scofflaws solve the disclosure problem by simply imagining that they will never have to provide a public account of their behavior. The odds of being caught and forced to confess are so slim. Politicians and business leaders have shown what to do if accused. Like Bernie Madoff and Bill Clinton, they simply say, "I did nothing wrong." No shame: no guilt. Research has shown that Sarbanes-Oxley has had no impact.

Secondly, transparency sometimes conflicts with privacy. That is why there are locks on the doors of public bathrooms. HIPAA regulations equate nontransparency with professionalism in some cases. Trade secrets, labor bargaining or contract negotiations are not expected to be revealed in ethical conversations. The confessional in the Roman Catholic religion and patient disclosure of full health histories would collapse if made public.

There is in fact a serious academic school of moral philosophy based on disclosure. Adam Smith, the Scottish thinker at the time of the American Revolution who wrote The Wealth of Nations, advocated for an ethics of moral sentiment. A key element in his system was the "impartial spectator." The moral test, for Smith, was to ask, "What would an observer who was completely knowledgeable of every detail of the situation, unerringly rational and perfectly impartial do?" The ethical individual is supposed to reflect from this perspective and choose as the impartial spectator would choose.

Smith is not so popular anymore. It's so hard to find impartial spectators. We — having limits on our knowledge, rationality and partiality — have difficulty recognizing what the impartial spectator would do. The default position seems to be, "Could I defend what I want to do if I absolutely had to?" That is hardly a firm foundation for moral behavior.

The nub:

❶ There is no impartial spectator; we are being silly when we sign up for that job.

❷ It is acceptable not to disclose information relevant to moral choices, provided that one can disclose the reasons for failing to disclose.

❸ The only person to whom 100 percent disclosure of factors in moral choice is owed is ourselves.

Writing About the Other Guy

I have come to expect that editorials will be about other people doing something they should not have done or failing to do those things that would make our lives easier. A staple in the genre is the ethics editorial. A little preaching to the choir never lost any preacher his or her job.

Scholars say the oldest writings (not the oldest events) covered in the Old Testament are in the Book of Amos. Actually, they are transcriptions of the chants the prophet sang in the gates of the cities of Israel. They are among the most powerful poetry I know. "Thus saith the Lord: For three transgressions of Damascus, and for four, I will not turn away the punishment thereof." This follows with some specifics about these other guys' poor behavior and the punishment they will endure. The same formula is repeated for Gaza, Tyrus, Edom, Ammon, Moab and other local bad actors. That is good stuff if you are into schadenfreude.

Several years ago, I was asked to speak on ethics at a conference where evidence-based methodology was being used to develop guidelines for dentists in a treatment area. If you Google "practice guidelines" you will find about 10,000 such position papers from various organizations telling practitioners in various health professions how they should do their jobs. This was to be another. The little research that has been done on such guidelines shows that somewhat less than half of practitioners in any area are aware of the guidelines that exist, and a small proportion of those who know follow them.

I talked about the ethical responsibilities of advising one's colleagues how to practice. The conference organizers thanked me politely but suggested they had had something else in mind. They wanted me to make a case that it would be unethical for dentists not to follow their guidelines. My personal view is that if they had wanted to engage practitioners they would have invited them to the meeting. Only the people in the room get to say what counts; we cannot do it on behalf of others.

I find four types of written pieces about ethics in dentistry. "Others are doing something wrong" and "our problems would be relieved if others did what they should" are the two most common. Scholarly work designed to explain how people behave ethically is scarce. Of the 18 journals of professional ethics, there are about eight in medicine, several each in nursing, law, business and other fields; but none in dentistry. The writing I am in awe of is where people stand up and say, "This is what I am prepared to do to make the profession better."

Amos cautions against pointing the moral finger. But you will have to look at verse 6 of his passage to find out why.

The nub:

1. Stop talking about what others should do.
2. Search for deep understanding of how people actually behave morally.
3. Declare what you are willing to do for dentistry.

Duty to Be Understood

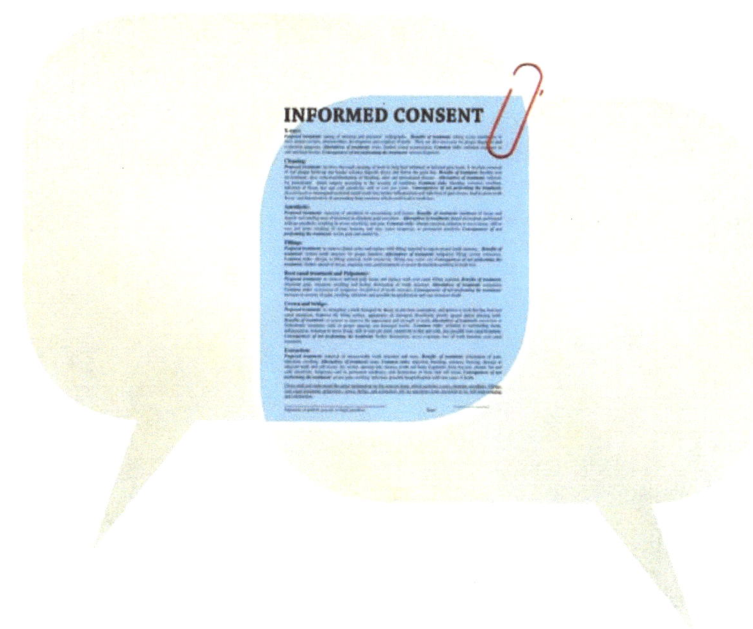
INFORMED CONSENT

My first mortgage agreement was on two legal-sized papers. The last time we refinanced, it took 45 minutes of robo-signing, and I think I am now suffering from carpal-tunnel syndrome. At one point, I balked. My wife, a former banker, said it was okay because one of the documents I had signed said if the bank was not really satisfied it could change things. There is hope for getting around this inefficiency. Now all we need is a click-of-the-mouse on the computer screen saying we agree with everything, whatever it is. Some of this is enforceable and some of it is not, but it has boosted enrollments in law schools.

New York City dentist and opera singer Stacy Makhnevich discovered this recently. She requires as a precondition for treating patients that they sign an agreement not to post negative comments on social media. Sometimes things go wrong, sometimes the office fails to manage the patient with a complaint, sometimes the patient lets the world know his side of the story, sometimes the dentist tries legal intimidation and sometimes the courts find in favor of the patient. Then the dentist is several hundred thousand dollars poorer and has a PR nightmare on her hands. Courts have always looked beyond the signature on the dotted line and declared some agreements unenforceable. It all depends on whether both parties understood what was signed, if they had the capacity to act based on that understanding and whether reasonable people would have signed.

I recently had some surgery and was "given" informed consent via the computer. I scrolled and read for about 25 minutes. The doctor was impressed, saying, "Gosh, you must have read it." He was further amazed when I gave him a page of notes about things that were illegal, unintelligible and simply misstated. The champ was the phrase "the patient may use ..." where the three letters in the word "use" had been misarranged.

From an ethical perspective, it is very simple. Patients give informed consent — dentists, staff, piles of papers and computers do not. The giving of consent is an act that signals patients understand enough about what is going to happen to them that they would not change their minds if they knew any more details. Of course, there is a "reasonable person" rule that sets a practical limit. A good check to see whether one has gone far enough to be understood is to ask the patient to repeat back his or her understanding of the key points. Having that in the charts is about as bullet proof as one needs to be.

The nub:

1. "I told them so and it is in the chart," plus good luck, are all that is needed to prevail in court.
2. Patients will always judge treatment experiences against their expectations. Informed consent is the place to make sure that the comparison will be positive.
3. Know what the patient expects before you try to give it to him or her.

Permission to Speak

As the old joke goes, "Do you mind if I ask a couple of questions?" "Not at all. What is your second question?" No one needs permission to tell others when they feel the profession is being damaged.

I recently received a copy of an ad placed by a specialist. It asked potential patients, "Why settle for less than a board-certified specialist?" I find that offensive. It implies that all others are less qualified.

But of course, there is more to the story. This ad is now notorious in various groups in organized dentistry. The conclusion, after months of consultation among members of state and national committees and with legal counsel, is that the advertiser is within his legal rights to make this sort of claim as a business proposition. "It seems," said one California dentist, "that the government has tied our hands and there is nothing we can do."

That is right and wrong at the same time. What is right and good about dentistry is not limited to the financial or legal dimensions. The advertiser is counting on winning the commercial battle, but he can only win the ethical battle if no one speaks up.

The offensive dentist's behavior cannot be controlled in this context, but he is morally constrained to recognize the obloquy of his colleagues.

Of course, one cannot libel others, but private expressions of honest professional opinions are protected speech. A message about how colleagues see the matter switches the focus away from legalisms to ethics. The Department of Consumer Affairs and the state boards do not limit what can be said about good dentistry.

How does one go about crafting an ethical protest? Here is an example.

Dear Dr. X,

I have seen your ad in such-and-such and am troubled by the claim that patients who choose your colleagues are "settling for less." You are certainly within your rights to make this statement as a commercial enterprise regulated by the Department of Consumer Affairs. My concern is ethical. It is possible to read your advertisement as implying that other dentists who are completely qualified to perform the procedures patients seek your services for are inferior to you and must be "settled for." Perhaps you were not aware that patients and your colleagues could interpret your message in this light. I am certain you will want to maintain the high regard patients hold the entire profession in and the ethical respect of your colleagues.

That is all. No exaggerations, no demands, no threats. A few letters from prominent dentists in the area should send the right message.

The nub:

1. There is both a commercial aspect to dentistry and a professional one. Dentists should care about both.
2. It is never necessary to request permission to express a position on ethics.
3. The payoff for speaking out ethically is to help define the profession. Controlling others is not part of the procedure.

Reputation Clipping

Have you ever wondered why dimes and quarters have little notches, called milling, around the edges? It is there to discourage clipping the coins. Back in the day, when a British pound was a pound's weight of silver, the unscrupulous filed or more aggressively clipped the edges off coins before passing them. Pretty soon, the pile of silver shavings was worth something.

That bummed out the first Queen Elizabeth who was a monetary conservative, and she proposed minting bright new money that would fairly boast of integrity. Her very shrewd financial adviser, Thomas Gresham, talked her out of it on the grounds of what has come to be known as Gresham's Law: bad money drives out good. Folks hoard the new money and circulate the old, clipped stuff.

The same is true for reputations, especially on the Internet. Everyone knows by now that slamming professionals is, for some people, a perverse passion, and for all a protected form of speech. Firms that "protect the reputations of professionals" cannot remove material from the Internet. They will advise you to have friends stuff the ballot box with nice comments, negotiate with the sites to see if you can get a placement higher on the page in exchange for "buying ads," and personally contacting grumpy customers immediately. (I would offer the same advice, and charge much less for it.)

When I was a director of a health care district board, I wanted to know more about HCAHPS (the patient satisfaction survey required by the Feds of all Medicare providers). I was interested in learning about the validity of the data collection system. For example, I wanted to see whether patients who said they had been fully informed about post-discharge routines had lower readmissions rates. Or do those who like the food live longer? My Internet search came up empty. I contacted the national firm that contracts to provide these data to most hospitals (Press Ganey) and found that they could only demonstrate reliability (patients answer consistently) and face validity (the questions look like they measure the right thing). No one seemed to understand the difference between answers that are consistent with other answers (reliability) and answers that related to health outcomes (validity). To the best of my knowledge there are no construct or predictive validity studies relating patient satisfaction to health outcomes for HCAHPS.

Gresham's Law guarantees that professionals will have their reputations clipped. There are two reasons. First, bad news travels better than good news. Righteous indignation is now a national pastime and our leaders in Washington are setting the example. Second, dentists are really very, very good at what they do. It is not news to be treated with safe, effective, health-enhancing techniques as well as respect and grace.

The nub:

❶ No news is good news. Outstanding care is the norm.

❷ Do not try to change people's minds; shape them at the beginning, especially while they are in your office.

❸ Never circulate clipped coins or reputations.

Smoking Guns and Targets

The nub:

All evidence is only partially valid.

Whether we use evidence of ethical conduct cannot be determined by which outcome we want to appear.

Confronting immoral behavior is an act of courage that involves morality.

Imagine that you are on trial, having been accused of being ethical. This is a bit surrealistic, but the question arises: is there enough evidence to get a conviction? You explain to your attorney that you have passed the state board's ethics test. She shakes her head. "We need to find a smoking gun, or perhaps a pattern of consistent behavior."

A smoking gun would be a single dramatic act. To make it bulletproof, it should have no mixed motives and look 100 percent volitional. Was that pro bono work for the patient's sake or bad debt repackaged as good public relations? In your heart, your intentions were pure. But the world is so likely to misunderstand.

Perhaps it would be better to go for a pattern of outcomes. Open your charts, gather testimonials, point to your clean record. There is power in trends, but not so much when they come after the fact. A few targets with bullet holes where they should be might be impressive. But any lawyer worth his or her fee would show that (a) a pattern of outcomes does not prove that a particular act caused it, (b) chance could produce almost any pattern if we looked hard enough and (c) selective evidence is suspect.

This way of looking at matters is annoying. If we begin with the assumption that the profession is perfectly ethical, this all seems like mean-spirited troublemaking. But perhaps others do not start from that position. Can we really use profession of an intended outcome to demonstrate that we have behaved as intended?

Now let's change the situation in just one small way. Imagine you are on trial, but this time accused of being unethical. There is the smoking gun. An undisclosed broken file in the sinus, an insurance claim for extracting a tooth that is still in the arch. "It was an atypical accident, a reporting error, a misunderstanding," you say. You can explain it away. Some dentists believe the ADA Code of Ethics says do not criticize other dentist's work because you do not know the circumstances under which it was performed. Not quite true. It says you should take steps to find out what those circumstances were.

But perhaps there is an ugly pattern. Insurance companies tell me they can name the dozen most unethical practitioners based on distinctive claims patterns. Usually these problems are made to go away privately because there is no smoking gun and state enforcement agencies are underfunded out of mistrust of effective government. The best defense against pattern detection of immoral behavior is to break the chain of evidence. Until we curb policies of nondisclosure and settlements that self-dissolve to prevent discovery of past wrongdoing, smoking guns and patterns will be weak stuff. ■

License to Practice

The following document is on display in the Baldwin Home in Lahaina, Maui, dated 15 July 1865.

It is decided to be proper that ____________ should act as a medical doctor, for under me, he having exhibited to my satisfaction his qualification as such doctor. Therefore, I hereby give my sanction to his practicing medicine from Hawaii to Kauai, so long as he obeys my directions and observes the laws of the King of this government, and conducts himself properly and honestly.

The following is the scale of fees to which I consent, if a cure is affected:

1.	Very great sickness	$50
2.	Less than that	$40
3.	A good deal less	$30
4.	Small sickness	$20
5.	Very small	$10
6.	Attending a friend	$ 5
7.	Incantation to find out disease	$ 3
8.	Taking case from another doctor	$10
9.	Certificate of a doctor	$ 3
10.	Refusal by the patient to pay	$10

The nub:

1. It is worth reflecting on whether there should be a CDT code for oral health value.

2. The fee schedule influences good oral health outcomes.

3. It is possible that there are practice code features that protect professionals rather than patients.

Notice that there are no ICD-9 codes. Disease is defined generically and subjectively. But observe the introductory clause. These fees are valid only "if a cure is affected." We have changed from an older philosophy of paying for health outcomes to paying for technical services rendered, regardless of their impact. It is also noteworthy that the old Hawaiian fee schedule allowed a charge for diagnostic services, though it is unlikely these days that insurance companies would pay for incantations.

Whom one treats matters. Attending a friend is a social obligation that can reduce the fee charged from $50 to $5. Tough practice, since "ohana" in Hawaiian means that almost everyone is your friend. On the other hand, taking a case from a colleague deserves a $10 bump. That would certainly be an anticompetitive incentive. The currently fashionable practice of patients "shopping on price" would certainly be dampened if a fee equal to treating a small case were added. This would never fly in today's courts, but it could encourage comprehensive treatment.

The opportunity to increase a patient's bill by $10 if he or she refuses to pay is a boggler. Somehow my suspicious mind sees the shadow of a lawyer friend of the physician in the background. "If I collect," says the lawyer, "I would not want to take the entire award from your share, my colleague, so let's add a little something so you can have some and so can I."

Finally, note whose authority a physician in 1865 Hawaii was allowed to practice under. The state only handled the legal and ethical part of the practice and the established members of the profession controlled who came in and how they were to be compensated. We still retain some of those features after 150 years. ■

The Proximal Surface of Morality

The nub:

1. No batting champion looks at the proximal (bat); they look at the distal (fence).

2. Good dentists guarantee good techniques; good techniques may or may not make good dentists.

3. No dental supply house sells good dentistry.

I learned to distinguish proximal from distal years before becoming associated with dentistry. Psychologists and philosophers use the terms to point to those things close at hand and under our direct control and to things we intend and strive for in the general and longer view. It is as if the proximal is the means and the distal the ends of our activities.

Consider the question: what caused the patient to get better? One answer might be "RTC with Thermafil following an evidence-based dentistry (EBD)-justified protocol." An equally good reply would be, "A particular practitioner very carefully treated the patient with wisdom, skill and caring." Both the proximal technical description and the distal explanation in terms of professionalism are correct. But there is a difference here.

Online publishing and the resurgence of commercialism in dentistry have brought about an avalanche of journals that promote dentistry as a bag of techniques. EBD is piling onto that movement with its semi-religious encomiums of scientific rigor. There are no journals that talk about what makes a good dentist. (Perhaps the implication is that one who "buys into" the latest techniques is the best dentist.) The literature identifies products and techniques by name and performs statistical tests to find which is best; dentists are counted in the journals as nameless noise in the statistical error variance, as are patients.

I have conducted research with colleagues that suggests this is a distorted way to look at it. Chambers, D. W., Leknius, C. and Reid, L. A general method for describing sources of variance in clinical trials, especially operator variance, in order to improve transfer of research knowledge to practice. *Journal of Prosthodontics*, 2009, 20 (1), 1-7, is one example. When fabricating a temporary crown, the nature of the operator accounted for one-third more of the variability in outcome than did the material used. Additionally, some practitioners could use either material and some could only manage with the best material.

It matters whether the dentist is fixated on making the right moves or getting the right outcomes. Technically excellent dental care is not the same as promoting the best oral health. I do not recall ever having seen a CE program that promoted oral health (as opposed to more advanced dental techniques). The ADA now has an ethics hotline. It is early in the game, but first reports are that the inquiries are mainly of the legal sort: "Would my colleagues disapprove if I failed to inform a specialist that I am having collection problems with a referred patient?" or, "Can I fire an assistant who tells patients negative things about the office?" So far no one has asked, "Do you have any suggestions for new things I could try to raise the overall level of oral health among my patients?" ■

Commercial Cover

The nub:

1. Look to commercial concerns only after completely satisfying all professional obligations.

2. "Others are worse" is an ethical dodge.

3. "Drafting," remaining silent while benefiting commercially from the cover provided by the really bad, is hypocritical.

For most of the 20th century, the industrial elite ruled over the poor of South America, often by getting favorable laws passed and sometimes using thug tactics. When the drug cartels came, the privileged class did not turn nice. They upped their game, buying better politicians and outfitting a paramilitary. In commercial competition, one group provides cover for the others.

When one airline raises its fares, others follow, often just short of matching. Each summer, hospitals hire a crew of consultants to survey what other hospitals are charging so that they can set their fees "competitively."

It is human nature and good business sense to be slightly ambivalent about competitors who are blatantly commercial and successful. If the rising tide lifts all boats, it is a very comfortable position to sit in a stronger second place while taking the moral high ground of gently complaining about the crassly commercial.

Dentistry is a business and a profession. Recently there has been a lot of grumbling about commercialism, especially about corporate ownership business models. I would have expected a massive, indignant repudiation of everything using dollars as the measure of what is good in dentistry. The silence is worrisome. True, the American College of Dentists has issued several position papers challenging commercialism and the intrusion of third-party values and the Academy of General Dentistry has also begun raising important questions. But the voice of the leaders in the profession could be stronger.

Dentistry is a regulated business like real estate, requiring a license from the state. In California, the Department of Consumer Affairs sets minimal standards for commercial enterprises. Removing the license of a practitioner who conspicuously damages patients is a difficult process, as the lawyers will remind us, because it deprives the bad actor of his or her livelihood. Removing a license for maximizing financial gain, as long as some minimal standards are maintained, would be unthinkable.

It is not okay to switch between commercial and professional standards to suite the circumstances. The profession sometimes campaigns for important patient benefits that happen to coincide with commercial interests for dentists. The legislature and the public have difficulty understanding which is the operative motive. Promoting fluoridation and other public health actions would be less ambiguously worthy. Some practitioners feel inoculated from ethical matters because they are following the law. The uneasy quiet of the profession on the dangers of commercialism could be interpreted by those with suspicious minds as evidence that all dentists are benefiting from standards that are drifting toward economic measures of success.

The American College of Dentists has a simple rule for removing the commercial cover on dentistry. Dentistry is answerable to two standards: a commercial one and a professional one. Where there is conflict, the professional standard takes complete precedence. ■

Disease and Illness

The nub:

1. Providers who know everything about oral disease may still not know very much about particular patients' experiences.

2. There is always a history and a future for a dental visit, and they are different for the patient and the dentist.

3. Our system is perversely incentivized because it focuses on disease, for a moment.

The patient has five- and six-millimeter pockets, mobility, through-and-through furcations, bleeding and mild pain on eating.

This is periodontal disease. The etiology and prognosis are known and fully described in PowerPoint slides. But the case may be different for the patient. "Somehow" it just started to hurt occasionally. The dentist seems to be implying that there is blame here. Money and pain and inconvenience are now involved. The patient is experiencing illness.

The facts of disease and illness are identical where they cross like a large X when the patient is in the chair. But the disease path has a different beginning and end from the illness path.

A disease is a prototype abnormality with an established trajectory and minor variations. The CDT code is the same, the textbook description is the same, the optimal treatment is the same, the reimbursement is the same. But each patient has a different and personal illness. The diagnosis may be heartbreaking to the executive who imagines herself the paragon of health. Of course, she will do whatever the dentist recommends and pay in full in cash, but a blow has been dealt to her self-image that extends well beyond the mouth. A down-and-outer who has not been to a dentist in 15 years might take it in stride. "What's the cheapest thing you can do, Doc?" What matters to the patient comes before and after the office visit, and identical visits do not mean identical illnesses.

Dentists are trained and experienced in managing the path of disease. Harvard Business School professor Michael Porter, who is something of an expert on health care policy, thinks that the biggest flaw in our system comes from following the disease path in diagnosis, treatment, financing, design of our offices and patient contact. That has contributed directly to high costs and poor and unevenly distributed health outcomes.

If we decided instead to build our system around health, we would focus on five points on the illness path. First is prevention and patients' willingness to participate in the health care system at all. Second is awareness of need and diagnosis. The third stage — the common one on both paths and often the only one we think of — is intervention in acute disease situations. Recovery and rehabilitation are the fourth phase. The final one is establishing a new "normal," one we hope is sustainable.

The American health care system focuses almost entirely on the cross point in the X. Cost can be read along the disease path and health along the illness path. The intersection of the paths is where providers can make the most money, but it is not where they can do the most good. ■

Ethical Principles as Smoke Screens

The nub:

1. Do not use ethical principles as smoke screens for practice that is self-interested.

2. Clever interpretations are for sale, but caveat emptor.

3. Ethical principles do not cure patients; moral dentists do.

It requires only a few minutes to learn the five principles on which the ADA Code of Ethics is based. It requires a lifetime to live them.

Respect for autonomy, beneficence, nonmaleficence (not causing others needless harm) and justice (fair distribution of benefits and burdens) are the traditional backbone of bioethics. The ADA has added a fifth: veracity, or not letting others entertain misconceptions to their detriment. There are others, such as integrity, continuous learning and trustworthiness.

Perhaps a few philosophers quibble around the edges about the principles, but dentists have nothing bad to say about the principles in the abstract. The issues seem to come in at the implementation stage.

4C in the ADA Code says that dentists should, as a matter of justice, report cases of consistent and gross bad treatment to the appropriate authority. But who knows all the details on the ground? The patient might have caused the problem or misrepresented it. Fair enough. Reasonable doubt about interpretation allows practitioners to endorse the principle without having to take any action.

Principles can wear many costumes. Is the ethical distribution of benefits and burdens one that favors the dentist or the patient or the insurance company? Or perhaps, in particular cases, the interests of the dentist and the patient together outweigh the interests of the insurance company.

Clever minds can manage potential conflicts of interest. Marc Rodwin's study, *Medicine, Money, & Morals: Physicians' Conflicts of Interest*, is a 400-page catalogue of the tussles between ethicists and lawmakers on the one hand and physicians on the other, as they battle over the commercialization of medical practice. Rules and laws are put in place to define and curb abuses; nuances and new definitions are created to get around the restraints. The principles are never in question, it is just a matter, as President Clinton observed, of what one means by "it."

The real course in dental ethics consists of finding out how one's colleagues interpret "it."

We are now losing ground as dentists turn to others besides their colleagues to craft convenient definitions of what counts. Lawyers have long made a good living finding justifications for questionable actions their clients take in their self-interest. Practice management gurus can only stay in business if their clients think they are successful. The powerful new player is the PR firm that represents dentists by designing websites, sending out press releases and handling the marketing front end for practices so dentists can concentrate on providing the best quality technical care. All of these folks who are helping the "new" dentists (I mean the ones with novel interpretations, not the young ones) are ethical in principle. So are the dentists who interpret principles to suit their needs. ■

The End of Ethics

When do dentists stop their ethical development? We have heard that perhaps dental school is the last chance. Some believe it is all over by junior high school because of family and cultural influences.

The answer, of course, is that dentists can stop ethical development any time they want. Arguably, a rare few become rigidly set in their ways at an early age. Perhaps they hide their primitive ethical code under some fancy lingo. It would be a complete disservice to the practicing community to say that the book is closed on ethical growth when professionals cross the stage at graduation.

The three main approaches to ethics in the Western tradition are all products of mature thinkers. Aristotle's virtue ethics — which is close to what we now call professionalism — was actually set down by his illegitimate son, Nicomachus. Jeremy Bentham's utilitarianism — the greatest good for the greatest number — was the labor of a lifetime. Immanuel Kant — who believed in the imperative of good intentions much like the Golden Rule — wrote his great work on ethics at age 61.

For many dentists, their most ethical years are still to come.

This question has drawn the attention of researchers. In the book, *Moral Development in the Professions*, James Rest and colleagues conclude that individuals continue to mature ethically as long as they continue to learn generally. As the Greek playwright Aeschylus noted, "To learn is to be young, however old." Dentists probably learn more after graduation than before. It is just the focus of learning that causes the concern. I regularly look at the C.E. offerings of the dental schools in California, state meetings and the big regional meetings such as Rocky Mountain and Chicago Midwinter. These provide a mirror of where the practitioners' collective attention is focused. It is not on ethics.

There are advantages in clinging to the misconception that ethics is fixed before dental school. First, this would excuse the need for engagement. If the other person is beyond the age of ethical plasticity, why bother to have the conversations? Certainly, the other would be wasting his or her time talking with me, one might say, as my values were set at an early age. This is a silly view to take — unless one is in a position of power and afraid to talk about alternative views.

A second advantage would be shifting the burden of training, mentoring and collegial interaction to selection. Sometimes it is said that schools have let the profession down by admitting students who have "nontraditional" values. That is a self-sealing indictment. There are no tests for ethical development that are valid for dental school admissions. ■

The nub:

1. In the fine print of the contract for life, it clearly states that all of us are responsible for our own ethical development and that this clause cannot be canceled at any point during one's life.

2. It also says we are responsible for the ethical development of our colleagues – throughout their careers.

3. Tomorrow, each of us could be more ethical.

Clinical Research

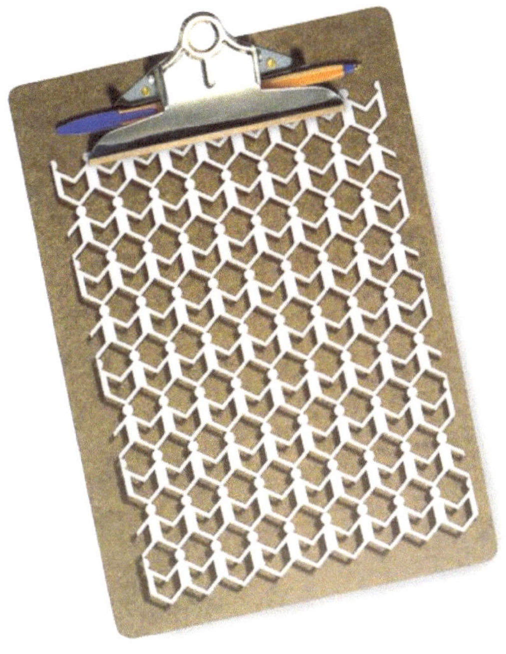

The nub:

1. Data for research and practice belong to patients.

2. Participants in clinical research must consent and recognize fair risks and benefits, and disadvantaged groups must not bear disproportional burdens.

3. Research and practice are privileges.

It may be surprising to learn that asking people in shopping malls what they think of water fluoridation is clinical research while using a calibrated apparatus to study the abrasive properties of a dentifrice or the sheer strength of an adhesive is not. It is a natural mistake to assume that "clinical research" means getting knowledge that will help the practitioner at chairside. Clinical research ethics is all about patients instead.

The definition of research is systematic collection and analysis of data for the sake of making generalizable public claims. When the Gallup poll reports that 58 percent of Americans trust dentists to have their best interests in view, that is research. When a dentist pushes back from a stack of charts in his or her office and concludes that it is time to start referring multirooted endo cases, that is not research because, although a generalization, it is not intended for public consumption.

What makes research clinical is the involvement of humans as the source of data. These contributions cover physical evidence such as biomarkers and assessment of treatment outcomes. They also include behavioral evidence such as reports of satisfaction, opinions or choice behavior.

The purpose of securing the mandatory prior approval of Institutional Review Boards is to protect humans who participate in research. The Nazi medical experiments that came to light in the Nuremberg Trials sensitized the world to potential abuses in the name of science. A short time later, there were revelations that prisoners in Tuskegee, Ala., where having treatments known to be effective in curing syphilis systematically withheld to scientifically gauge the effect. This was a vulnerable population being exposed to unreasonable harm without their consent.

In 1978, a report was issued that established the rights of human research subjects and, indirectly, the rights of all dental patients. Google the "Belmont Report" and read it. The report established three principles. Respect for persons means participants must give fully informed consent. Beneficence means there must be a clear preponderance of expected benefit over risk and risks must be minimized. Justice means vulnerable groups such as the poor, prisoners, children, the handicapped and pregnant women should not bear unreasonable burdens and that the privileged should not benefit at the expense of the less privileged.

If these principles sound vaguely familiar, it is because the Belmont Report provided the foundation on which the ADA Principle of Ethics is based.

The purpose of ethical review of clinical research is to honor the contribution of participants to the accumulation of knowledge. Researchers are not "entitled to" free access to data. Just so, dentists are not "owed" the opportunity to perform the highest quality of care they are capable of delivering — that privilege must be granted by one's peers and by individual patients. ■

The nub:

1. Power is often a substitute for ethics.

2. We may have had enough of soapbox ethics.

3. Those who are most likely to bring ethics to dentistry are dentists.

Should Ethics be Peer Reviewed?

There are approximately 75 ethics journals published in English. Bioethics is the largest specialty focus in health. Medicine has five journals. The professions are well represented, with multiple journals in business, law, education and nursing, and specialty publications for ethics in agriculture, engineering, research, the environment, information technology, media, sports and the military. A typical single issue of the *Journal of Business Ethics* contains 200 pages of peer-reviewed, referenced papers quarterly.

But there are no journals for dental ethics. *The Journal of the American Dental Association* began publishing the "Ethical Moment" in 2006. But the title suggests something less than the kind of in-depth discussions that would build a discipline. The Academy of General Dentistry and some other journals give advice. Ethics is a favorite topic for editorials, especially of the "we should all do better" type. The *Journal of the American College of Dentists* has a journal-within-a-journal called *Issues in Dental Ethics* and has been the richest source of writing about dental ethics, with an average of 40 pages of material each year.

There are two troubling characteristics of the literature on dental ethics. The obvious worry is the small amount of detailed and cumulative thought being given to the topic. Additionally, the articles typically address ad hoc issues, often with ad hoc opinions about how the writer would respond. It might be accurate to characterize much of dental ethics writing as well-meaning personal opinion rather than scholarship.

A study in one of the management ethics journals may shed some light here. In the research, individuals were given an ethical dilemma, and the outcomes of interest were how certain the decision-makers were regarding their choices and how much they consulted those affected by the decision. Decision-makers' sense of power was subtly manipulated. Subjects first took a management quiz and a "high technical sense of power" group was created by giving falsely inflated feedback on the results. A low power group was created by faking poor scores.

Subjects who mistakenly believed they were powerful (about management) were less likely to consider the views of others and were more confident in their choices (about ethics).

Dentists are high-powered folks. They pretty much define what is so in their day-to-day worlds. Medicine is hospital based; business and law are played out in give and take among equals. Professions where expertise is open to frequent, knowledgeable scrutiny are more likely to have ethics journals.

Likely, we can begin to expect to see some journals in dental ethics. Group practice and corporate dentistry are growing. I recently polled informally a dozen leaders in dentistry and asked about the big ethical issues in the profession today. None mentioned patients; no one said anything about staff. All comments were about differences of opinion regarding how dentists should treat each other. ■

Does the ADA Have a Code of Ethics?

The nub:

1. Know the ADA code inside and out – follow it.

2. Ethical principles are general justifications for what is done, but incomplete and sometimes inconsistent guides for choosing the right action.

3. One can practice in perfect harmony with one's peers and still be regarded by the public as missing the moral mark.

No. I read what we commonly think of this way every six months because it is a foundational document. However, what I read is the *American Dental Association Principles of Ethics and Code of Professional Conduct*, with advisory opinions. Three documents — none actually a code of ethics.

The Principles of Ethics contains very brief statements and definitions about autonomy, nonmaleficence, beneficence, justice and veracity. Pretty much everyone knows these now. They provide rational justification for a range of behaviors, often contradictory ones. Philosophers call such statements "thin claims" because they are academic and admit of multiple interpretations. Ethics should be a mutual understanding among all those affected — dentists, patients and the public — about what is in their common best interest.

The operational part of the ADA document is the Code of Professional Conduct. Here is where we find the patterns of behavior expected of dentists, such as truthfulness in representing one's qualifications, not splitting fees and the obligation to report gross or faulty treatment done by other dentists. It helps to remember that it was originally known as the Code of Etiquette.

Professionalism is an agreement among members of a professional group about how they expect other members of the group to behave. The code was created by and is amended by a vote of the House of Delegates. It covers behavior among dentists (the bulk of the ADA code) and behavior toward patients. No patients participated, as far as I have been able to determine, in the creation of the ADA code. Such documents are supposed to represent to the public what can be *expected of any* ADA dentist, and they serve as standards for what any ADA dentist can expect of his or her colleagues. The Principles of Ethics are aspirational; the Code of Professional Conduct involves provisions for sanctioning or removing ADA membership for those who are in violation.

The third part of the ADA code consists of advisory opinions. These apply to the Code of Conduct, not the Principles of Ethics, and only some of the items in the code have advisory opinions. The opinions are more detailed language, often examples, guiding the interpretation of the code. For example, in 4C (Justifiable Criticism), it is stated that when alerting patients of problems related to work done by a previous dentist this "should, if possible, involve consultation with the previous treating dentist(s), in accordance with applicable law, to determine under what circumstances and conditions the treatment was performed." Often the code is misunderstood as saying that one should refrain from commenting on what others have done because the circumstances are not known. The advisory opinion makes it clear that the dentist who sees problems should try to find out what is behind them. ■

Virtue Epistemology

Are you the dental student who prepped for National Boards with DentalDecks and "released" exams, or did you carefully review your lecture notes? Did you put passing behind you or follow up on your weak disciplines? The distinction turns on something called virtue epistemology.

The ancient Greeks had three primary terms of knowing (we use understand, comprehend and so forth rather loosely). *Techne* means "know how." *Episteme* is "know about." *Phronesis* means "know why" or wisdom. Dental practice requires a solid mastery of each, and an insufficiency in one department cannot be offset by brilliance in another. In dental school there were cases of impressive performance in the lab or lecture that failed to transfer into the clinic.

For the most part, philosophers have left *techne* and *phronesis* alone and concentrated on what we sometimes call didactic knowledge — what can be tested for C.E. credit in the journals. In fact, the branch of philosophy devoted to studying how we know anything at all is called epistemology. The subspecialty of virtue epistemology is about the ethics of what we say we know.

Cheating on exams, plagiarism and misrepresenting one's qualifications are just plain unethical. Trying a procedure you think *might* work, "shading" a report about what your heard, skimming abstracts rather than reading articles and shoddy Internet searches are examples of breaches in virtue epistemology. So is using old exams and not following up on feedback that one's discipline knowledge is spotty. Poor virtue epistemology is about accepting sloppy thinking for the real thing.

The current concept of "virtue" is different from its meaning in virtue epistemology. We moderns say a heroic act was virtuous because it represents praiseworthy, self-sacrificing behavior. The old Greeks had something more like habits accepted in the community in mind. Acts were not virtuous, people were. Virtuous behavior was what one expected of colleagues because knowledge was a shared resource. Knowledge has intrinsic rather than instrumental value. Finally, virtue was not one's best score; it was typical performance. Virtue epistemology would be the habit of approaching knowledge with the same sort of care, deep curiosity, integrity and conscientiousness that we hope to see in the best examples of dental professionals.

In the 1990s, the accreditation standards were changed to require that schools teach about ethics. The most recent change has been to mandate both humanism (treating all with dignity) and critical thinking. The methods of inquiry appropriate to professionals must now be taught in dental schools. The old model of students listening and watching passively while faculty performed that was presumed to come to a magical end on graduation day is being replaced by making students full members of the inquiring community. This is a move to virtue epistemology. ■

The nub:

1. Others care about what you know, or say you do.
2. Do not say things are so just because you want them to be.
3. Take the same care and pride with what you know as you do with the fabrication of a crown.

The World Is Coming Apart

Ukraine is dividing into segments because each part thinks it can do better on its own. South Sudan broke away from Sudan so as not to share the oil. Now South Sudan is in danger of being divided between the Dinka and the Nuer, neither wanting to share. States' right is eroding this country at a pace that is beginning to resemble the 1780s or the 1850s. Cliven Bundy is his own country — his rules, his benefit. And membership in the ADA has dropped by more than 15 percent since I started writing about ethics.

This phenomenon is called moral hazard. It works like this: Groups exist because members have a better chance collectively than they would alone. But sometimes a localized opportunity appears for individuals to get temporary personal advantage by withholding participation. They defect strategically. The result is that those remaining have to pull a heavier load. That stimulates further defections. The centerpiece of the Affordable Care Act is an effort to curb moral hazard by preventing insurers from cherry-picking who they cover and keeping citizens from cherry-picking when they seek coverage.

Why is moral hazard growing in popularity? Globalization, mass and instant communication that gives identity to splinter groups and overall prosperity are good reasons.

The Swiss economist Ernst Fehr and his collaborators have performed many experiments where participants play games that depend on cooperation. These are called common good games because players do better when they regularly and predictably build the pool of shared resources. Each member of a small group starts with a small gift of cash. They decide how much to invest per round and receive a payout based on the total invested by all players, augmented by a bonus from "the bank." The enhanced fund is divided equally among all players. In typical experiments, a pattern quickly emerges where some try to take advantage of the common good by claiming a share without contributing. In such situations, groups shut down the game and no one wins.

The problem can be fixed. Allowing agents the option to spend some of their own resources to punish those they regard as selfish boosts the community's flourishing. Effective communities all have some such mechanism where individuals pay into a pool to enforce the rules. Taxes are needed for courts and police as well as investment in infrastructure. Cities that have water meters have substantially lower water rates.

Fehr shows that investing in the public good is worth it if moral hazard can be controlled. When secrecy is stopped, when defectors must bear the cost they impose on the group and when selective participation is curbed, the net return to all participants (including former defectors) typically increases by about fourfold. ■

The nub:

1. Moral hazard is a cancer that saps groups of their potential to share the benefits of cooperation.

2. It can be reversed by transparency and willingness to call those who are taking too much from the common good.

3. Join the ADA.

I Never Lie

"The Cretans are all liars;" this according to Epimenides who lived about 600 B.C. and was himself from Crete. We no longer worry about such silly word games. Today, everyone lies. A lot. In one study where people exchanged stories, the lying rate was four per hour. Men are about two or three times as mendacious as women are, the former tending to bend the truth for self-enhancement and the latter for self-protection. No one teaches children to lie, but all of them are pretty good at it by about age 4. Functional MRI research has located this habit in the anterior cingulate gyrus and parts of the prefrontal and premotor cortices.

Sometimes we even speak untruths about lying. The prince of principles, the philosopher Immanuel Kant, said that civilization would be impossible unless people always told the truth. The facts do not support him on this. The biblical injunction is not against lying. The "thou shalt not" is about not lying about lying (perjury).

It just will not do to define lying as making claims that do not correspond to reality or to say that it is always wrong. "False and misleading" is generally determined by a group of 12 people specially assembled and painstakingly advised. We can add enough qualifications and special circumstances to make almost all but the most cockamamie statements true. Companies have lawyers who specialize in this sort of thing. "Skin Wonder Magic Cream makes my skin feel years younger," the gorgeous 18-year-old purrs. But that is not false or misleading because *she* might really feel that way. A politician is a person who specializes in saying things he or she knows are not so.

Not all lies are created equal. "White lies" make society better. "Grey" ones promote the interests of the deceiver without hurting others. Only the "black" variety of lie is dangerous. This is the false framing that promotes the interests of the deceiver at the expense of the person deceived. What is bad about lies is using them to hurt people who are defenseless against them.

There are five principles of ethics recognized by the ADA. One of them, veracity, is not usually included among the cardinal four ethical principles by bioethics. About 40 percent of the Code of Professional Conduct is devoted to restrictions on what dentists are supposed to say about themselves. The sparks fly in this area because dentists know when a colleague is making or implying an unjustifiable claim. But patients are the ones who are defenseless. The point of any professional code is that misleading the public is easy for professionals but damaging to the profession as a whole. A better definition of veracity than telling the truth would be never leaving others in a position where they could have benefitted from additional information. ■

The nub:

1. A lie is a dangerous tool, not a sin.
2. Facts can mislead; we must look to the effect on others.
3. Deceiving oneself is also known as "stupidity."

How Much Is a Gored Ox Worth?

There are two ways to handle damages. One is based on who is right; the other is based on fairness. We tend to use both methods, depending on which better serves our interests.

The patient approved the provisional. It says so right there in your notes. Now there is a complaint about color match and the bite is not exactly right. As the tussle goes on and other parties are brought into the discussion, the patient seems to have recalled that the dentist was "abrupt and condescending, perhaps so much so that informed consent was compromised." Which is better: standing by one's principles or looking for some common ground?

Lawyers and economists tend to divide on this issue, with lawyers urging that their clients purchase all the right they can afford. Economists are generally inclined toward rational division of the pie. Philosophers, including ethicists, come down unambiguously in both camps. Warning: choose your advisors carefully!

Ronald Coase (rhymes with rose) won the Nobel Prize in Economic Sciences in 1991, based on what may be the single most widely read and cited paper in economics: "The Problem of Social Cost," *Journal of Law and Economics*, 1960, 3, 1-44. The case he dissects goes something like this: A doctor expands his practice to include sensitive diagnostic testing. The factory located next door installs equipment that causes vibrations that interfere with the doctor's testing. The doctor estimates that the vibrations are costing him $20,000 per year in lost business. He has the option of moving to a new location at a cost of $10,000. On the other hand, the factory could either move (costing about $75,000) or install vibration mitigation barriers for $5,000.

One approach is to go to court in hopes of getting a judgment. If the decision goes against the factory, the doctor would be awarded $10,000 and the factory would pay court costs and lawyers' fees. If the decision goes the other way, the doctor loses $20,000 and additional costs are piled on accordingly. Either way, somebody loses a lot and the lawyers prosper.

There is another approach based on justice rather than rights. The doctor could give the factory $5,000 to install mitigating measures. This would be a savings of $10,000 for the factory and $5,000 for the doctor (the $5,000 paid out subtracted from the $10,000 needed to move).

Coase's Rule is that governmental regulations and court decisions should mimic as closely as possible the solutions reasonable people would have negotiated. That is a good rule for people as well, even if it would put some lawyers and philosophers out of work. ■

The nub:

1. It is unethical to force third parties to guarantee our rights when we can secure them ourselves.

2. If we sometimes choose rights and sometimes choose justice, neither is a primary good.

3. Our image of who we are, what we are entitled to and the recognition of others are precious, but not without cost.

Supreme Court Weighs in on Dental Ethics

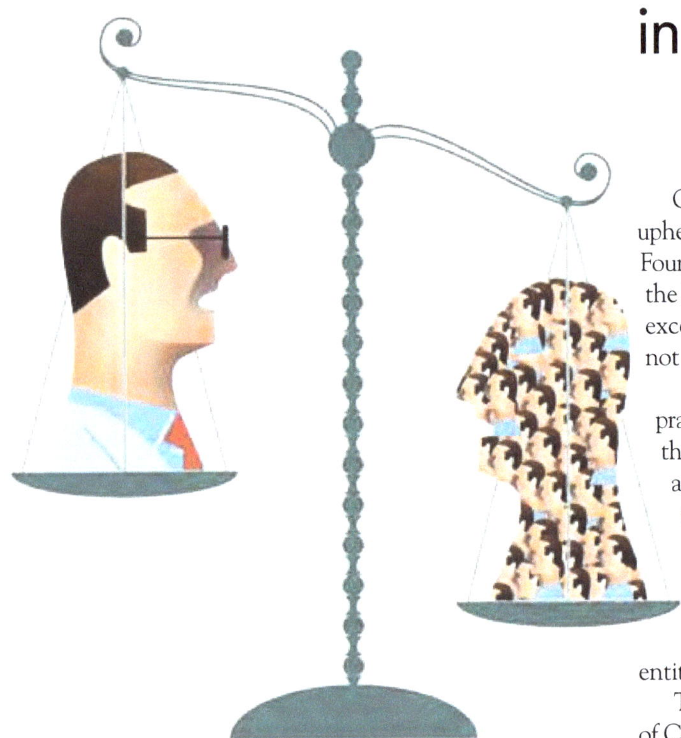

The nub:

1. The U.S. Supreme Court favors fair competition in the public's interest.

2. Anticompetitive regulations are acceptable as long as the public, not the profession, has the final say.

3. It is clearly expected that dentists' ethical code takes precedence over legally allowed advantages.

On Feb. 25, the U.S. Supreme Court, by a 6 to 3 margin, upheld the decisions of an Administrative Law Judge, the Fourth Circuit Court and the Federal Trade Commission that the North Carolina State Board of Dental Examiners had exceeded its authority in ordering teeth whitening establishments not owned by dentists to cease and desist operation.

Teeth whitening is not mentioned in the North Carolina practice act, but a committee of the board determined that it had the authority to enforce an anticompetitive action to stop nondentist teeth whiteners. They argued that these actions are appropriate because the board is an agency of the state, authorized to craft, interpret and enforce regulations governing the practice of dentistry. The issue was not the board's authority to regulate practice, but whether it can do so as a sovereign entity, independent of supervision by other state entities.

The basis for the appeal was a 1984 decision allowing a board of California raisin growers to fix prices. The *Parker* precedent [Parker v. Brown, 317 U.S. 341 (1943)] contains two standards: regulations must be clearly articulated as state policy and the agency's actions must be actively supervised by the state to ensure a chain of authority reaching back to the public. Such supervision must include substantive as well as procedural review by representatives of the state who are not active market participants and who have the power to veto or modify the agency's actions. "The Court holds today that a state board on which a controlling number of decision makers are active market participants in the occupation the board regulates must satisfy … active supervision requirements in order to invoke state-action antitrust immunity."

Now for the ethics. The Supreme Court recognized a professional board's right to regulate practice such as dentistry, including the establishment of anticompetitive restrictions where appropriate. What it restricted was a board's privilege of doing so independently. The principle of state sovereignty gives ultimate authority to the citizens and allows the administrative apparatus of the state to create and enforce rules on behalf of the public. But the chain of accountability cannot be broken by allowing an agency to function in the interests of a class it represents without verifying that such actions are also the interests of the public at large.

The board also argued that unless it is allowed an autonomous voice, it would be difficult to recruit professionals willing to serve on behalf of the public interest. This drew a bit of moral scolding from the court: The preamble of the ADA *Principles of Ethics and Code of Professional Conduct* was cited as calling "upon dentists to follow high ethical standards including honesty, compassion, kindness, integrity, fairness and charity." ■

I, IT, THEY, WE…

A Grammar of Ethics

Parsing logical sentences and distinguishing one ethical philosopher from another probably compete for last place among the exciting things to do on a Sunday afternoon, right up there with untangling the wires for the stereo system and alphabetizing the canned soups in your pantry. There is a reason — after we have done it, no one can tell the difference.

Here is the connection between grammar and ethics. First-person ethics is an academic exercise. Third-person ethics is gossip. Speaking about ethics in the second person almost never happens. Some things we say about ethics never get out of the "I" voice. Some sentences point fi ngers at "they" or "it." After we have done it, no one can tell the difference. The precious cases begin, "We …"

It is very hard to think of an example of ethics that is entirely private. Almost per defi nition, to count as good or bad, what we do has to affect others. So should the solution. There is a danger in mistaking a one-party solution to a two-party problem for a sound, two-party ethical resolution.

The real annoyance is third-person ethics. "*He* should be doing …" "Did you hear how *they* are overcharging, misrepresenting, underdiagnosing, patient stealing and all the rest? Makes one sick." There are three parties in these third-party grumblings: Dr. Righteous, the friend of Dr. Righteous who is listening and "they" (who are generally only spoken of in their absence). As a rule, "they-ness" is easier to spot the less "they" look like the friend of Dr. Righteous.

It is easier to tell others how to act when one is standing on a pedestal or wearing some sort of ceremonial garment. Avoiding the possibility of having a conversation also helps.

Sometimes we clean up third-person ethics by removing the personal dimension. We shift from "they" to "it." "It would be best if everyone …" "It is obvious that …" "It stands to reason or everyone sees the wisdom of ..." The "it" arabesque also seems to elevate the conversation to universal principles. Neat and clean, perfectly fair, just do the right thing. It only shows up in the very fi ne print that certain individuals are allowed to interpret which "it" is the right one.

The defensible position is the second-person perspective. You and me. We may not agree about which philosopher has the grand insights, but there is a better chance of walking out of the room in agreement than if I insist that you agree with me before you can sit down. ■

The nub:

1. Private virtues are only ethical when they make others' lives go better.
2. Third-person scolds and ex cathedra judgments are sham ethics.
3. We can only fix it when those involved sit down and talk about it.

Ethics Sweepstakes

The Fourth of July parade in Sonoma is a favorite of locals and tourists alike. It *is* America. An hour and a half is quite a statement for a town of about 15,000 – political candidates, vaqueros on horseback, the health care district board, martial arts and dance studios, the teen-center youth, the fire department and three local theater groups.

There was also a banner carried by two women proclaiming an antifluoridation message: "When in doubt, leave it out." And there were two dental offices.

Here is a little ethics test: Which groups were out of place in the Fourth of July parade? As painful is it may seem, I would rule out the commercial interests – the two dental offi ces, the bank and the plumbing outfit.

I am in favor of public water fluoridation. I have testified about its benefits, especially in increasing the number of days children remain in school. I know better than to engage antifluoridationists in debates over (pseudo)science. There is not enough common ground between us there for two people to stand upright.

But even when I am right, I have no right to muffle the voices of others. There is a sad story about a New York dentist who attempted to charge a patient $100 for each day a negative posting remained on one of those rating service websites. She said he signed an "informed consent" declaration surrendering his right to make negative comments. The courts saw matters the patient's way.

So are dentists just supposed to turn the other buccal mucosa? Sure, professionals should stand up for what is clearly known to be in the best interests of the public. But that is exactly what did not take place in the parade in Sonoma on the Fourth. The dental profession stayed away in very large numbers from marching in support of a safe, simple and effective way of improving the health of a lot of kids in the Valley while some touted their own reparative services.

The ethical misstep in this situation is the false belief that we must convince the other side we are right before an ethical action is possible. When we adopt the view that others must agree with us before we will talk about how to go forward, we cut off possibilities. We make enemies rather than progress. A winner-take-all ethical sweepstakes has a preset number of winners and all the rest are losers.

We are best served by making our case in positive terms and excusing others from following if they are only faking it. We do not need to change the minds of antifluoridationists. But we should be marching to inform the public in general. ■

The nub:

1. Agreement on ethical principles is not a precondition for moral behavior.

2. Moral maturity is not a matter of knowing the right answers, but how to handle disagreements.

3. Sentences that begin with "yes" have a better chance of making a soft landing.

Autonomy and Agency

The nub:

1. Respect for autonomy is nice, but a bit paternalistic because either party alone can make that determination.

2. Dentists and adult patients and nonpatients are agents, with the capacity to affect each other.

3. Morality requires that the same moral status as agents be accorded all concerned.

Yogi Berra had it right: "If the people don't want to come, nothing can stop them." They are autonomous, in the literal sense of the term "self-governing." Dentistry is one of the professions that has made quite a bit out of this principle. Patients get to choose … even if the choices are limited for their own good.

Bioethicists ground informed consent in the norm of respect for autonomy. Sometimes informed consent is mistaken for a legal process. Sometimes it means little more than making certain patients have a generally favorable idea what is going to happen to them.

Respect for autonomy is an ethical pillar in most professions. It just makes sense that when the professional sets up the ground rules, patients should be allowed the opportunity to opt out.

But this is only half the story. What if we looked at it from the perspective of potential patients? It is plausible, if a bit uncomfortable, for others to set their own conditions on whether or how they will participate (or not) in health care. This is a free choice and involves no necessary prejudice against the professional, even if it means a hit to prestige, income, lost time and a ding on the self-concept of serving the public. Others show "respect for autonomy" by not forcing conformity. Respect for autonomy loses some of its nobility unless we accept that it works both ways.

Agency is a sturdier moral concept. Agents have the capacity and responsibility to affect others by their actions. Both dentists and patients are agents. Patients are agents when they refuse radiographs, choose less-than-ideal treatment to remain within the limits of their insurance coverage or decide not to go to the dentist at all.

Each dentist choice affects both the patient and the dentist; each patient choice affects both the dentist and the patient. Dentists and patients are (potentially) reciprocal moral agents. The challenge is to find a common way forward that neither party would have any reason to change.

In the traditional approach to ethics, dentists consider only what they understand to be in patients' best interests and claim the moral high ground by reluctantly allowing them to elect less than ideal care. The dentist's interests have been screened off from consideration as not belonging to the sphere of professional ethics. Not so, of course, for patients who judge their own and the dentist's advantage.

Morality requires more than one person deciding whether he or she has done right by private standards. Professionals justify their standards by roughly conforming to what their colleagues are doing. Morality requires that agents recognize the valid claim of other moral agents to affect them. ■

Ring of Gyges

Here is a 2,500-year-old myth that bears on the question of whether humans can ever be trusted to do what is right for their own sake. The story is told in the second book of Plato's *The Republic* by Glaucon, Plato's brother. He was trying to convince Socrates that morality is a social construct and if it were not for fear of being found out, we would all break the rules when given a chance.

Gyges (pronounced GUY-geez) was a shepherd in Lydia who discovered a ring that made its wearer invisible when turned a certain way. Gyges used the ring to seduce the queen and together with her kill the king, and then he became king. Glaucon argued that what holds us back from wholesale immorality is fear of being discovered in our improprieties and thus losing our reputations.

If the plot sounds vaguely familiar, you should think of the Oxford don who studied philosophy early in his career and eventually wrote the blockbuster trilogy, *The Lord of the Rings*, JRR Tolkien.

Socrates essentially ignored Glaucon's challenge, saying instead that those whose reason rules their passions will not be slaves to their passions. Not a very convincing argument for folks like Hitler whose reason ruled him in a twisted way. Socrates resorted to name-calling: those who do not act the way he wants them to are being unreasonable.

The nub:

1. Beware of rules that guarantee too much freedom from observation.
2. Peer review and informed consent can be our friends.
3. A moral world is necessarily constrained.

Daniel Aeirley is among the recent researchers who provide evidence for something like a ring effect. In a typical experiment, individuals are allowed to take a short multiple-choice test on trivial facts (such as the average annual rainfall in Nepal). The tests are unsupervised and self-scored. When finished, participants collect a small cash payment based on their self-reported scores. Those who are allowed to take their tests with them or shred them consistently take, on average, more reward than those who just leave their test — with no name on it — on the unattended desk.

Cameras used for issuing automatic tickets to drivers who run red lights are being removed from cities. There are two arguments against the system: first, if they cost the city more than they take in, they are wasteful of public funds and second, if they bring in more than they cost, they are gouging the public. As most drivers are unaware they are being watched until they get a ticket, they find it insulting to have had their supposed invisibility violated.

Very likely, the case is that each of us defines a personal zone of moral safety that we carry around with us. Some of us need larger zones than others, and all of us recognize the necessity of shrinking or expanding our license for moral discretion depending on the circumstances. We have our very own little, adjustable rings of Gyges. ■

The Cost of Ignorance

Dentists and lawyers bill differently. Fee-for-service means that an MOD is charged at $150, regardless of whether it was easy or difficult or whether it was done well or poorly. Lawyers bill by the fraction of an hour, regardless of what they were doing during that time. I have always fretted that neither system is quite right, but I know of no practical way of capturing value added.

What particularly irks me about lawyers is that they learn on the client's nickel. I have to pay for an attorney to study precedents and get smart about the applicable law. I think patients would be skittish of a dentist who says, "I really have never placed an implant in the zygomatic space so I will have to read the literature on that topic. I figure I should charge you about $750 for that."

Dentists are supposed to know or refer. But dentists do need to update their knowledge and there are costs associated with this. The ethical issue is who should bear these costs.

Health care professionals generally have three ways to update their knowledge: the literature, their own experience and advice from peers and commercial sources. Research on physicians has shown that the most powerful influence, measured in terms of propensity to change practice behavior, is the latter. Going to C.E. courses to hear what experts think about the literature they have read or the results they have achieved on atypical patients is not inexpensive. The hall talk is often invaluable as a way of finding out about what ads and studies do not report.

In my own research on innovation among practicing dentists, the No. 1 lever for self-improvement is trial and error. I have nothing particular against trial. And if we could use a kinder term, "difficulties" or "small and correctable unexpected outcomes" are actually very valuable learning opportunities. There is a sort of "secondary wisdom" that guides the primary learning. Negligence, malfeasance and obsolescence are some of the terms we use to describe a shortfall on this wisdom about the imperative for continuous self-improvement.

There is an old story about a curmudgeon who kept the power plant in a small town going until he retired. Four months after the new guy showed up, the whole system went down and all the obvious fixes were ineffectual. The veteran was called back. He looked things over, took a huge wrench and wacked the machinery. That worked great. The city fathers were grateful, but none too pleased with the bill at $501. "For beating the thing with a pipe," one politician complained. "I want to see an itemized bill." The reckoning came: "Hitting machinery: $1; knowing where to hit: $500." ■

The nub:

1. Knowing what you don't know is valuable.

2. Finding out about what you don't know is a professional obligation.

3. The patient should never bear the cost of what you don't know.

The New Autonomy

Privacy protection, informed consent, blocking public health initiatives and moral hazard arguments (why should I pay into a pool for benefits I need less than others do?) have pushed "right to autonomy" into the center of public attention.

On national television recently, gang members in Florida who specialized in robbing high-end homes bragged that they used Google Earth to plan their break-ins. They were five times referred to as "the alleged robbers" and they pleaded "not guilty." That is a level of sophistication in separating the glory of a national TV spot from its consequences every lawyer would admire.

The average American surrenders massive amounts of personal information at the click of a mouse, but opposes collecting any data that could possibly be used unfavorably. Government resources are to be targeted to the most efficient use, but profiling is illegal. Quarantines, mandatory vaccinations and evacuation orders in the face of forest fires are resisted even by those who find them perfectly reasonable.

The proper term in philosophy is "respect for autonomy," not "right to autonomy." The origin is two Greek words "auto" and "nomi," meaning "self" and "rule." The value runs deep in America, with its strong Anglo-Saxon and Germanic heritage. The Magna Carta was not a guarantee of benefits to the common person. It was a protection for the minor nobility from arbitrary laws imposed by the king, who, after all, was French, not English.

In the 1820s, debates in England's Parliament veered toward high-tone public character assassination. Broughton said Channing was an "ass," but that gave Channing no right to take offense. It was as though inflammatory comments were safe when placed in "scare quotes" — if you know what I mean. A cub parliamentary reporter named Charles Dickens ridiculed this nonsense in his first novel, giving us the term "Pickwickian." It means wishing to be taken seriously only by those who agree and to be immune from judgment from those who do not agree. Social media posts are flagrantly Pickwickian. In fact, much on social media is just cheap self-promotion, sometimes even complete with a Pickwickian legal disclaimer at the end.

Perhaps dentists only have a Pickwickian right to respect for their autonomy. Informed consent is mutual agreement between professional and patient — double autonomy. This exits when it is accepted that patients can judge dentists, when dentists must stand behind every implication of their positions. Perhaps with the best of intentions, dentists have officially muddled this notion. Claims about "putting the patients' interests first" are meant to advertise a higher calling and justify unquestioned trust through selective messaging. Of course, such slogans are not expected to be taken literally. Saying so and then reserving any escape clause seems to be wanting to have it both ways and to undermine respect for autonomy. ■

The nub:

1. You cannot protect what you are willing to give away.

2. Anything a dentist says is an irreversible procedure.

3. Wanting only to be heard "in a favorable light" is asking too much.

The Ethics Awards

The nub:

1. Beware public awards (advertisements) for "being ethical."

2. A definition of ethics as not doing anything contrary to code is unremarkable.

3. The Behavior that Makes the World Better Prize can be claimed this afternoon.

We are going to have a big black-tie event with a posh location, elegant food and lots of media coverage. Well-known presenters will read glowing narratives and present prizes. We will honor the most ethical among us.

Something does not seem quite right about this picture. These sorts of things actually happen, but it gives me a funny feeling. Ethics is not in the category of things we seek public credit for.

Last year, I received an email blast announcing that a dental manufacturer had been honored for its ethical standards. The award was given by a consortium of other dental manufacturers, ostensibly for the purpose of touting the high ethics of those dental manufacturers who contribute to hosting the prize. And I recently got an email alert that this winner was being sued for price gouging.

During the 17 years I was academic dean, we witnessed an escalation in awards for publicity. I love graduation, the celebration of accomplishment, the pride of parents and the optimism of entering a profession with a fantastic future. Only the graduates should be on the stage. But other causes are muscling their way forward. We had offers from the International Academy of Overtreatment and the Garage Full of Stuff Supply Company. Every specialty, including some I am unfamiliar with, offer certificates suitable for framing and one year's free subscription to their journals. They also furnish a half-page background statement they expect will be read during the presentation.
Art Dugoni was wise enough to pass on most of these.

Can you imagine an insurance company hosting a breakfast honoring dentists who submit fewer than 2 percent suspicious claims during a year? Or hanging a sign in the waiting room that proclaims, "I have treated all my patients as well as I could"?

Charity and service deserve to be recognized, but not ethics. The problem, of course, is how can we promote ethics unless we take advantage of the thoroughly American practice of combining advertising and public recognition?

There is a solution to the problem, but it involves a better defi nition of ethics. Too often, we settle for "ethics" as not doing anything contrary to the code. That certainly makes ethics a taken-for-granted non-event. No prize for that.

Here is an alternative. Ethics (I prefer the term morality) is the behavior we collaborate with others in for the sake of making the world better. Every beautiful crown, oral cancer diagnosis, heart-to-heart meeting with a straying colleague and component society meeting attended is a moral act. It makes a better world for the one who does it and the one who receives it.

As to the matter of awards, the prize is the better world … immediate, unavoidable and valuable. I hope all your lives overfl ow with ethics awards. ■

The Dilemma Dilemma

The nub:

1. Do not confuse sophistication with soundness.

2. Because one has a right to do something does not mean that it is right to do it.

3. A good name for a questionable practice is still questionable.

America continues to make impressive progress in the field of PC superlatives. This goes beyond renaming our ignorance. I have something more serious in mind such as free-range lettuce or gluten-free spam filters. A good name on an ambiguous practice does the trick. We live in a world of mind-numbing adverbs that tell us more about how we should feel than what is really so.

My current favorite in dentistry is "evidence-based." Rough translation: "I think there are some published studies that meet some protocol requirements that support what I want to do in my practice." We used to just say, "There are good reasons for doing what I am doing," but "evidence-based" sounds so much more sophisticated. And it is short code that can be slipped easily into conversations, and it is understood that it is a bit impolite, except in academic settings, to ask for a detailed explanation of the research evidence.

For many of the same reasons, I am not a fan of "ethical dilemmas." I hear the term most often when someone wants to signal that he or she is wrestling with important and complex decisions. It is a way of indicating that the speaker is serious about ethics.

A "lemma" is a standard proof that can be inserted in a logical argument without having to go through all the detailed steps. It is a prepackaged thought sequence that removes the need for actually working things out. A "dilemma" is a situation where one lemma justifies one conclusion while another justifies a different course of action.

Ethical dentistry rarely involves dilemmas. Overtreatment, upcoding, biased informed consent and shoddy work are not dilemmas. Most often, ethical issues turn on whether one has the courage to do what is clearly needed.

Often dilemma talk is about finding a justification for a tricky situation with a possible but shaky option. A dentist may choose to focus his or her practice on high-end patients who need primarily elective and nonhealth enhancements based on the principle of respect for autonomy. Letting people choose what they want (dentist and patient) is one of the five ethical principles promoted by the ADA. The principle justifies the practice.

One might object that there are other principles that are being overlooked. Beneficence (promoting the good of others) and justice (the fair distribution of benefits and burdens) come to mind. Now we have a trilemma. But we do not have a solution. How can we decide which justification takes precedence? The ethics experts say we should make an informed decision based on a "balance of the principles." This means that there is a superprinciple that lets us decide what the right balance is. No one knows what that superprinciple is, but we have seen people use it. ■

A Cry for Help

I am one of those very peculiar men who regularly asks for directions when driving. I believe in the African saying, "If you want to go fast, go alone. If you want to go far, go together."

But my system is failing. I find it harder these days to get help. As a country, we prefer to sell solutions instead of answer questions. It seems it is becoming unfashionable in America to help others.

Part of the reason was obvious when I signed onto my computer this morning. Several minutes of protecting myself against unwanted spam put me in such a negative mood I had to pump myself up to be civil to those who were asking for my help.

Of course, I do need help from time to time with my computer. Very occasionally, I will go to the IT department at the school where I teach. They are knowledgeable when my number eventually comes up in the cue. I am much more inclined to chat informally with one of my colleagues. There is a person in HR who is a wizard with Word. A new faculty member in the basic sciences is a master of graphics. I prefer the users to the experts for several reasons. First, they are almost always able to help immediately, e.g., when I need the help. Second, they know the context of the problem I am trying to solve and help me with the problem I should be working on instead of the one I asked about. Third, they make certain I understand the answer rather than taking my computer and changing something so it no longer misbehaves in exactly the same way. I believe the same is true for dentists who recognize that they face ethical issues: they would prefer to get help from a colleague rather than from an academic expert. And for the same reasons.

In an article in the February 2015 issue of the *Academy of Management Journal*, I read about helping behavior in a software engineering firm that uses teams to develop projects. Among colleagues who were expected to help each other, 26 percent of the email requests for assistance and 28 percent of the phone calls for help were ignored. OK, I have a better record than that. However, the computer has become an all-purpose labor saving device. Just ignore inconvenient requests.

Calls for help are more successful when begun by establishing or reaffirming existing social relationships. Another way to boost success is to explain why it matters to the person from whom help is sought. Acknowledging the status of the helper is useful. Finally, only a tiny fraction of requests for help that are made in person are refused. ■

The nub:

1. Social fatigue is damaging our willingness to help others.

2. Help is more likely to come from one who shares your problems than from experts.

3. No one cares how much you know until he or she knows how much you care.

Kahe

As with all Hawaiian words, *kahe* is rich with overlapping meanings. The root idea is "flow," but the term also means water in a stream or the changing tide. It means almost any mass noun composed of parts whose movement conforms to the contour of the land. Continuous, natural motion and progress are also part of the concept.

Kahe is an excellent strategy for ethics. We seek to be where we should be and we flow around the obstacles to getting there.

Too often, the conflict is framed as either "smash the evil" or walk away. Insurance refuses to cover what you know is the optimal care, so condemn it. A colleague starts running ads belittling all other dentists because they have not had the "advanced training" she claims, so complain. Poor children are not receiving the oral health care they need because Denti-Cal reimbursements are "unethically" low, so we stomp our feet.

The face of ethical challenges is constantly changing. If we keep staring at them from the same perspective, their features will only become more intractable. But if we work around them, they begin to look different. This is kahe. Morality is a process not an event.

Kahe may sound soft, like passive council for quietism and turning one's back on vigorous ethical action. Not so. Energy spent being upset is not the same as energy spent getting to where we need to be.

It is a nasty trick we play on ourselves when we exaggerate the magnitude of an issue in order to give ourselves a reason for not trying to fix it. And here is the surprising thing: any action taken is likely to change the nature of the problem. Sometimes two or three partial actions are necessary. Remember it is a stream of life, a constantly emerging new set of opportunities where each step one takes changes the prospects. The boulder in the middle of the road may look entirely different as we pass it by on the side.

There is also an internal psychological dimension to kahe. The pop psychologist with the impossible name of Mihaly Csikszentmihalyi has amassed convincing evidence that professionals and other masters of their craft experience a transcendent state when they are effortlessly performing at peak levels. He calls it "flow." Some people have never experienced ethical flow.

The dominant view is too often one of ethics as a struggle to impose our concepts of right and wrong on a world we see as evil. A fitting term for this might be the "ethics of righteousness." We "fight the good fight," "work to uphold standards" and "decry corruption, abuse, selfishness, mendacity, deceit, greed and anything else that benefits others by means we would not use." ■

The nub:

1. Do the best possible every day in ethics; the best possible is the most ethical.

2. Flowing toward the best possible may open a clearer understanding of better opportunities.

3. Solve the problem you are given or reframe it; don't let the problem define you.

Are Physicians Really That Unethical?

The nub:

1. The term "ethical" is often used in a loose sense.

2. It takes time to grow into unprofessional practice habits.

3. Overgeneralizing based on thin evidence that supports one's preconceptions is ethically problematic.

About 350 California physicians, of 105,000, have their licenses disciplined each year. A widely cited 2005 article in the *New England Journal of Medicine*, "Disciplinary Action by Medical Boards and Prior Behavior in Medical Schools," seemed to place the blame on young practitioners and medical schools. The paper is frequently quoted among leaders in dentistry and dental education, even by those who have not read it.

The California version of this paper was published in 2004 by Maxine Papadakis and colleagues in *Academic Medicine*.

Between 1990 and 2000, 70 graduates of a California medical school were disciplined. The academic records of these physicians were collected and coded, along with the records of 196 colleagues matched by year of graduation and specialty who had not been disciplined. The sources included admissions information, supervisor notes on rotations and dean's letters of recommendation. Those with any mention of "concern" were placed in one category and those free of all concern were placed in a different category.

Logistic regression showed that physicians who had their licenses disciplined were twice as likely, statistically so, to have at least one note of concern in their medical school file. The researchers did not report the proportion of false positives (concern in school but not in practice) or the false negatives (concern in practice but not in school). Also not reported was the number of students dismissed from school for ethical reasons.

One interpretation given to this research has been that professional schools are falling down in their responsibility to identify, teach and screen out those now entering health care who may have unprofessional values. That depends heavily on what a license is disciplined for and what constitutes a concern over professionalism in medical school.

The most common reason of record for licensure trouble was negligence (38 percent). Various forms of unprofessional conduct, such as fraud, accounted for 27 percent. Many licensure issues (35 percent) were "failed lifestyle" matters, such as personal drug abuse, sexual misconduct or mental illness. Notes of concern about behavior in medical school also tended toward personal and social behavior: "student seems immature," "needs reminders," "disagrees publically with faculty," "talks too much in class" and "nervous during admission interview."

"OK," I have heard some say, "this is not strong evidence, but at least it alerts us that we should be looking at the schools and the young folks coming into the profession as a moral concern." Actually, if anything, the evidence suggests just the opposite. The average age of California physicians whose licenses were disciplined between 1990 and 2000 was 54. This is closer to retirement age than the beginning of independent practice.

As historian Mark Stoler notes, "History does not change, but our interpretation of it does depending on what has happened to us in the meantime." ■

The Invasion of the Memes

Your office is almost certainly infected with memes. They like to gather on the desk in the front office and many varieties are found chairside. They have even been found in the reception area, and parking lots, if you have one, are just one big meme. Infection control and OSHA standards offer no protection. In fact, they are memes themselves. All dentists work for memes. The CDA is a meme, and one of its most active branches is the publication you are holding in your hands at this moment or looking at on your screen.

Genes have been with us for about 3.5 billion years as templates for controlling the transmission of physical characteristics. They explain the fact that humans continue to live even while no individual human makes it much beyond 100 years. Memes have been around about 50,000 years, and they work pretty much the same way. Like genes and viruses, they are packets of information that cannot sustain themselves or reproduce without a host. But neither can the host reproduce true or act consistently without the information in its genes and memes.

Social media and selfies are memes. So are Labor Day barbecues and church attendance. When a colleague shows up at a professional meeting wearing the wrong clothes or without the report scheduled for discussion, we joke that he or she "must not have gotten the memo." What we mean is that she or she did not get the meme.

Evidence-based dentistry is a meme. It is a pattern of behavior, transmitted by contact with carriers such as colleagues, conferences and journals. It is a mutation that jumped species from epidemiological researchers in medicine. It briefly invaded management research and practices, but is now almost extinct there.

Corporate dental practice is another meme. It is a variant of the "mall practice" meme that appeared in the early 1980s. It is more successful in its current form because of supportive host factors. Federal policy has multiplied onerous regulations on small businesses and subsidized oversized student loans. Mature as well as new practitioners are defining dentistry exclusively as technical work. Outside capital and control and mass marketing via social media recruit patient hosts.

Organized dentistry is a meme. Although it is not fashionable to comment on this, membership numbers, participation rates, an increasing income gap within the profession and identification with nontraditional "nonprofessional" organizations are part of the new meme mix.

Professional ethics is also a collection of memes. These are passed from generation to generation as patterns of behavior. Whether traditional professional ethics remains a viable meme, becomes one of several options or retires as a topic in lectures on the history of dentistry will be decided by whether the dentists who have that meme continue to flourish. ■

The nub:

1. We do not have habits; habits have us.

2. Memes do not serve out ends; they use us for their survival.

3. Dental ethics is a meme subject to possible mutation and extinction.

Free-Range, Gluten-Free, Eco-Friendly Advertising

A friend of mine, who is very proud of his heritage, reminds me often that the Italians know the secret to long life: just eat spaghetti for 100 years. I recently read a cereal box that boasted a full helping of the product, with a cup of whole milk, supplies most of the minimum daily requirement for vitamin D.

Some of my colleagues and I have been working on a research project to see how dentists read the literature. Rather than ask authors or editors, we give practitioners a journal article about an innovative way to make a composite provisional and videotape them as they react to it. The article has lots of photos and is universally regarded as demonstrating an outstanding result. It is from the *American Journal of Esthetic Dentistry*, a rigorously peer-reviewed publication that accepted no advertisements, and is now out of publication after about three years.

Standards in the medical literature call for detailed documentation of products by brand name and manufacturer in publications to permit replicability, create an impression of attention to detail and advertise products for sale.

The most common reaction to product mention of the readers we have studied is suspicion. We hear the opinion that the literature (and C.E. presentations) often list product names connected to advertisements and to compensation for authors. Sometimes our readers thumb through the journal looking for a disclaimer at the end of the piece or advertisements placed near the article. Even though there is no evidence of such connections in the article we use, readers want to make a point they are on guard against the possibility of this effect.

Another common attitude is that product placement, even in the dehydrated formal style found in most publications, is a distraction. Dentistry is becoming product sensitive rather than technique sensitive. As one reader remarked, "I know most of these products, I have my favorites, and they're all about the same anyway."

A couple of readers were cautious of this type of article in general. "What general dentist needs to be instructed in how to make a provisional? This particular example is outstanding and beautifully documented. The point is not so much to inform as to demonstrate the technical superiority of the author. This is how you establish your pecking order among the elite on the C.E. circuit. And there is a difference in the honoraria one can charge depending on where one is in the pack."

A few readers took a different attitude toward product placement. "I used to be worried when I saw products mentioned prominently in clinical articles. But now that I have started lecturing, it doesn't bother me as much." ■

New and Improved!

The nub:

1. Regardless of one's attitude toward product promotion in publications, one's own words must be defensible (see 10C in the CDA Code of Ethics).

2. There is no way to avoid participation in the value exchange of American commercial culture.

3. One's opinion about product placement is dependent on where one is in the system.

Mrs. Jellyby and the Hot Rock

"Think globally, act locally." The first part of this popular phrase seems a bit vague; the second part is trivial. If your friend said he had decided to only hug the people he could actually reach, you would wonder whether he really got the concept.

Perhaps the greatest send-up of this concept is Charles Dickens's classic *Bleak House*. In the chapter on telescopic philanthropy, we are introduced to the Jellybys, a magnificently dysfunctional family of a voiceless father and an uncertain number of kids, all ill clothed, sick and infantile. One daughter is an alcoholic and another elopes to escape serving as her mother's slave. Only Mrs. Jellyby has it together. She is the doyen of the East London Branch Aid Ramification, a charitable group devoted to bringing Christianity and Western economic civility to the Borrioboola-Gha people in Africa by getting London soft hearts to donate funds for a coffee plantation and a factory to turn piano legs. Mrs. J. is the center of a network of communication that involves getting and sending hundreds of letters a day and distributing bundles of flyers for the cause. She is a force for global change. But the oldest daughter says, "It's disgraceful. The whole house is disgraceful. The children are disgraceful. I am disgraceful."

Now for the hot rock. Imagine dropping one in the shallow end of a friend's swimming pool. A minute or two later, you will find that the temperature of the rock and all the water is the same. Perhaps immeasurably higher, but that certainly will not last. This is the second law of thermodynamics, also called entropy. In any closed system that allows interchange, the trend is inexorably toward homogeneity.

This is one of those laws that cannot be broken. But we can get around it. The easy, short-term dodge is to build barriers that divide the hot from the cold, separating the haves from the have-nots. The more productive means is to make the system open — to expect and encourage new energy, hope and resources from outside the system.

Both accommodations have their shortcomings. Building personally profitable protective enclaves will add stress to the system and it will eventually collapse. Trying harder from within must be continually maintained and will never lead to large sustainable change. The effect of the hot rock (the heat coming from outside) will be greatest and most lasting on the water immediately contacting the rock. A smaller change will be caused by that hotter water that warms the water immediately next to it, but cools some in the process. The water at the deep end of the pool remains unaffected. The most effective counselors for Alcoholics Anonymous, domestic abuse, drug addiction, community development and good oral hygiene are those who live close enough to touch them. ■

The nub:

1. All change is within reach.
2. No one changes the system or others without being changed themselves.
3. Change is not sustainable without infusions of energy from outside.

Small Stuff

Before there was Watson that blitzed the experts on "Jeopardy," and even before computers regularly humbled chess masters, there was Arthur Samuel and his checker-playing computer. That was 1949, and Samuel probably had to hand-crank his machine.

Samuel started by giving his gadget some great tactics, such as jumping an opponent or getting to the king row. He had the computer assign high point values to the big payoff moves. At each move, the computer searched a modest range of available options and picked the one with the most points. The machine was allowed to adjust the point distribution. Following each move and the opponent's response, the computer would re-evaluate the approach and adjust point values. That was the learning part.

At first, Samuel pretty regularly beat the computer. But it got better and eventually Samuel had to give up the contest as being hopeless.

What did the computer learn that made it so effective? Mostly it was the small stuff. Open a space toward the middle rather than the edge of the board, reduce the opponent's possible moves, that sort of thing. Most checkers games are won or lost in the scrum at the beginning, based on slight adjustment in balance. After establishing control of the territory with multiple very small wins, even a 6-year-old child can run the board with kings and triple jumps.

The nub:

1. The small stuff matters the most in dental ethics.

2. It is easier to bend a green twig than move a mighty oak.

3. There is something everyone can do this afternoon to improve the ethical tone of dentistry.

And so it is with dental ethics. Disciplined licenses, lawsuits against unfair practices, Medicaid fraud and the like may get the headlines. But it is the daily, nuanced decisions — winking at a colleague's questionable dealings or causal depreciation of the aspirations of auxiliaries — that establish the tone of the profession.

A few years ago, I tested this idea, and the results have been published. I looked to see what effect we could get by having enforcers, such as state boards, clamp down on devious practitioners. I also looked at the relationship between dentists who are ethically upright and unafraid to point out the behavior of the few bad apples and the dentists who are ethically upright but decline to get involved.

Like Samuel's checker-playing computer, the real action depended on the small stuff. The relationships among good practitioners and how willing they are to put the details of good practice on the table were more important than what was done to the devious few. The effect is many orders of magnitude in favor of daily details.

The next time someone tells you not to sweat the small stuff in dental ethics and wait until something really big and important comes along, you can be pretty sure the person you are talking with has been waiting a lifetime for the right opportunity to do something ethical. ■

Informed Consent

The nub:

1. Because people want to know what will happen to them, they demand more pieces of paper: because CYA does not satisfy this need, more paper will be needed in the future.

2. Ethical informed consent is for standardized, "reasonable" patients following theoretical principles.

3. Moral informed consent takes place between two individuals mutually satisfied that additional information is unlikely to change the course of action they have decided on.

Informed consent now comes in three flavors: legal, ethical and moral.

For many, informed consent means getting signatures on documents no one reads but everyone understands are meant to protect the service provider. This is legal CYA, strongly endorsed by the insurance industry and sometimes nimbly stepped around by the legal profession. Staff has been delegated to "get" consent, and computers have made this as easy as a click here and a click there. As patients are assumed to be identical, one form fits all.

When I last had oral surgery, I was placed in front of a computer, everyone left the room and I emerged 20 minutes later with a list of questions that troubled the staff. Chief among my concerns was the phrase "patients may *use* various functions of the clinic . . ." The problem was that the word "use," although it had the right letters, had been jumbled in an unfortunate manner.

The ethical approach to informed consent is grounded in the principle of individual self-determination. Patients should be allowed to freely choose what happens to their bodies, time and wallets. The problem is that there is a wide discrepancy between what dentists and patients know about biology and dental procedures. So the patient has to be "informed." There is equally a gap between what dentists and patients know about what patients fear and value. So the dentist has to be informed.

The usual standard is the "reasonable person." Ultimately, those who stand in for a reasonable person are 12 lay individuals guided by attorneys. The research evidence is overwhelming that patients can accurately recall only a fraction of what they have been told, even a short time later. There is also good evidence that practitioners "steer" patients toward treatments the practitioner prefers by selective emphasis or omission of information. There has been little attention paid to whether patients are providing all the information needed for safe treatment.

The moral approach to informed consent is built on mutual commitments. A person consents to an informed decision when no reasonable new information is likely to change the decision. A dentist is about to start an extensive reconstruction case. Is there anything the patient might say that would change the treatment plan or the approach? "I am hypertensive and hemophiliac." "I have left my last three dentists after two appointments each." "I have no money." The same calculus is appropriate for the patients. "You should know the success rate for this procedure is about 90 percent, but I have never done one myself." "Yours is a very extreme case of this condition." ■

Friends in High Places and Others

The nub:

1. We like those who have the capacity and interest to do us good.

2. We ignore those who cannot help us and defend against those who are capable of doing things contrary to our interests.

3. If we only walk with those who are there to help us, we will generally be behind or in front of the crowd – but not "with it."

Who do we want for patients, for friends, as allies for the organizations we invest our time in?

Imagine a 2-by-2-foot table with "good/bad for me" on one dimension and "influential/benign" on the other. It should be obvious that we cultivate the powerful and friendly, avoid those who can potentially harm us, smile on nice little people and ignore the rest.

What a joy to have a few friends who are in a position to do us some good.

Those with little prospect of mattering receive little thought. We save a lot of time and energy that way. Those with small influence but presumed positive attitudes are our context. We "like" them on Facebook. We acknowledge their compliments and ignore their requests if inconvenient. They are frequently the objects of charity. We count on them, often in the aggregate. They are ideal patients. They have financial resources, time and availability, billable needs, networks of friends for referrals and capacity to show appreciation. In fact, that is the very definition of a patient: one who agrees to the conditions of treatment.

We do not have a name for individuals who need dental care but have not agreed to the terms of treatment. These should be classified in the influential, but not very supporting quadrant. They include the patient who insists on care that the dentist knows is less than optimal, insurance companies, those who post negative ratings, young dentists who want to change what it means to be professional and owners of corporate chains that place commercial interests above professional ones.

This is the troubling cell — the one where interests that do not align with our own are advanced by people who matter. It says a lot about our character how we respond. The philosopher Isaiah Berlin suggested that there are two common patterns. The hedgehog curls up in a ball, leaving nothing but hard bristles to ward off attack. This defensive posture is favored by those who perceive that they hold a better hand than they are likely to get if the cards are shuffled and redealt. The fox, the other approach mentioned by Berlin, fusses around looking for a rational perspective on the matter. The great American advocate of pragmatism, William James, makes much the same distinctions, but he places the elements on a time continuum. First, we ignore the powerful and unfriendly and then we push back. The third phase in this process is to claim that the change was our idea in the first place. ■

If Your Life Depended on It

Do you do any of the following?

1. Place an implant in the zygomatic space.
2. Spend 15 minutes answering a nervous patient's questions about a treatment decision after making the case presentation.
3. Upcode insurance claims.
4. Volunteer for CDA health fairs.

Now for a slightly different question: *Can* you do any of the actions listed above?

This is not an ethics test; it is an illustration of the Peter Pipe Pedagogy Principle. I met Pipe in 1969 when he was in much demand in the emerging Silicon Valley scene as an industrial trainer. He advised companies about establishing training programs for their high-talent employees. It was his opinion that companies like Hewlett-Packard were wasting money teaching people to do things they already knew how to do, but did not feel were worthwhile.

Pipe argued that we only have a training problem where people cannot do something when their life depends on it. Take another look at the four tasks above.

Dentists do not need courses in avoiding overtreatment, protecting the reputation of colleagues while ensuring that patients' health is not endangered, declining fraud, staying away from false and misleading claims, misrepresenting qualification and the like. Personally, I would find it a little demeaning if I were required to take courses or read articles about these sorts of things.

Where a little training can help is pointing out the boundaries. Is there a version of fee-splitting that gets around the standard prohibition? What do other dentists in my community do about justifiable criticism? What are the IRS triggers for an audit? These are practical and legal question, not ethical ones.

Professionals use a four-level system developed by Donald Kirkpatrick for classifying training. At the bottom are concerns about the participants' appreciation of the course. "Did the speaker seem knowledgeable?" "Was the topic of interest?" "Were the pastries fresh?" This is the level required by CERP for C.E. programs in dentistry. The second level requires a test of knowledge, usually a passing score on a written examination. Level III looks to see whether the course material has been incorporated into practice. Is the new material or method actually being used? The top level in training is measured in terms of outcomes. Is the recementation rate down? Are patients more satisfied with their care?

In dental school, didactic education is Level II. By the time students graduate, schools have shifted to Level III. There is discussion with continuing competency and portfolio licensure of moving to Level IV. Most ethics training is at the lowest level. ■

The nub:

1. Ethics training is needed only in cases where one cannot do the right thing if his or her life depends on it.

2. "Ethics" training is often a search for how far one can test the limits.

3. The ultimate test for good ethics teaching is whether patients are better off.

Hawks and Doves

The nub:

1. A likely way to lose a fight is to consider only your own position.

2. Bullies should be made to pay as much as we can extract from them.

3. Do not mistake pacifism for morality.

Most human interactions are "win-win" or close enough so we do not even recognize there are moral issues involved. But several engagements are so remarkably different they have names. One is "hawk and dove."

Here is an example. A dentist steps outside the bounds of professional conduct by blatant fee-splitting, improper delegation, deceptive advertising, overtreatment and inadequate infection control. "So what are you going to do about them apples, Buddy?" It won't go away by being ignored or by bellyaching. State enforcement efforts are time-consuming, vastly underfunded, uncertain in outcome and messy.

The guys with the black hats are bullies. They are playing hawk for all it's worth. Those with the white hats, the doves, have two choices. We can be hawkish as well, signaling our willingness to go to the mat. Or we can hide somewhere and claim we are taking the moral high ground by being righteous and not attacking the other. The bully has two choices as well: back down or double down.

There are four possible outcomes. A pitched battle that damages one or both parties and some innocent bystanders is the worst possible outcome. Believe it or not, the next worst outcome is for both sides to pretend there is no problem. Innocent bystanders are also hurt when the profession overlooks despicable practices by those calling themselves dentists.

As counterintuitive as it may appear, the best strategy (for everyone) is to begin the fight with lots of publicity, to pursue it as far as practical and to have a good exit strategy. The key to making this work is to understand the guy in the black hat's position as well as your own.

There are numerous research studies showing that when bullies are punished for taking more than their fair share, everyone benefits, including the bullies.

The reason we so often misplay hawk and dove is that we get doctrinaire and refuse to fight unless we are guaranteed a win. The trick is to have a good Plan B and know when to use it. Recognizing when to bow out gracefully as you discover your case was not as clean as you thought, switching to a different strategy or accepting a partial victory are good examples. It is also valuable to have some seconds standing by. In gang cultures, affairs of honor, tribal warfare and the American legal system, the second is usually a third party who is weak and unable to participate directly in the confrontation. A priest, one's mother and nonprofit public agencies are good candidates.

Assume that the black hat already has done these calculations.

Disabling the brakes and chaining the steering wheel in a game of chicken is foolhardy. Not facing those who compromise the reputation of the profession is cowardice. ■

The Well-Taylored Dentist

The nub:

1. Meaningful work can be divided into isolated and perfectible tasks and (sometimes) reassembled into efficient wholes.

2. Efficiency is not effectiveness.

3. Defining dentistry in technical terms may damage it.

Every MBA student learns about Frederick Winslow Taylor, although he is no longer held in great respect 100 years after his heyday. Taylor wrote the book on how to get the most out of workers. It was titled *Principles of Scientific Management.*

The Industrial Revolution had only gone so far in standardizing interchangeable parts in the assembly-line process. It was Taylor's contribution to standardize the worker. Taylor was the original "time and motion" guy. Famously, he determined the ideal size and shape of a shovel to maximize the amount of coal a worker could move in an hour. It has taken the health professions years to catch on to the notion. Until the professions caught on recently, consultants did well pointing out "best practices" one office at a time.

Taylor would have approved of CDT codes but been uneasy about the concept of oral health. The job of the boss was to discover which products sell at the greatest margin, break tasks into components and optimize them, move each task to the lowest paid worker possible and market and perhaps resell the package.

One can certainly imagine that Frederick Taylor would endorse corporate dental practice — but not the idea of a dentist or group of dentists contracting with a DSO to handle the backroom tasks of payroll, billing, compliance with regulations and the like. Taylor would have favored the corporate model with nondentist equity interests that treat professionals as production units.

Owner-managers of corporate practices have insisted that they do not interfere with technical dental work. That is correct. They make a good case for demanding technical acceptability of all work performed by employee dentists. But, dentistry is more than technical procedures, no matter how well done. Decisions such as which procedures are rewarded, what equipment and staff are available for various procedures, where practices are located and what hours they are open, and comprehensive care from a dentist who has a long-term relationship with patients are all part of dentistry, even though they are not "technical" in nature.

The true battle developing in dentistry is over whether dental care can be defined in isolated technical segments. I agree with William Sullivan of the Carnegie Foundation that the gradual death we are witnessing across all professions is due in significant part to the professions defining themselves in strictly technical terms rather than patient service.

The term "scientific management" was not coined by Frederick Taylor. He borrowed it for the title of his book. The first use was made by Supreme Court Justice Louis Brandies in his ruling on the Eastern Rate Case in 1910. The unions were suing the railroads that were pulling in large profits by repackaging the work of employees into commercial bundles of isolated technical units. Brandies ruled that, that was nothing but good "scientific management." ■

The Argument from Perfection

The nub:

1. Making perfection a requirement may mean missing out on the best available.

2. Blocking others from exercising their best option is being a 'dog in the manger.'

3. The current market for red herrings is much higher than it should be.

At the city council meeting last night, the elders listened patiently to a parade of people who were pretty convinced that the whole world is a conspiracy and to half a dozen dentists whom I found more reasonable. Ignoring both groups, our leaders decided to send a letter to the county requesting that the state law on water fluoridation not be applied here.

I had worked out the math on savings in state funding for local schools associated with water fluoridation reducing absences at $2.5 million per year in the country. But one council member was having none of that. He produced a can of Coke from under the dais and asserted that surely we would be better served if kids would just stop drinking soda. I suppose he is right, but he was not proposing that the council do anything about reducing soda consumption.

What is wrong with this argument? Logically, nothing. Practically, everything. Academic philosophers have a technical term for this kind of reasoning; we call it dumb. Colloquially, it is known as a "red herring." When riding to the hounds was the thing in England, the most sporting gentlemen gave the fox a chance by sending out their staff to drag strong smelling fish, herrings if they could be found, to confuse the dogs. The basic tactic is to substitute an important but insoluble problem for a solvable one that is being opposed. Result: It kills the practical small gain and accomplishes nothing. And all the while, the politician does not have to go on record as opposing the measure he or she is working to defeat. It is widely believed that there are a lot of red herrings in the Potomac and Sacramento rivers.

It seems as though a wise person is making a rational choice between two alternatives: fluoride or curtailing sugared beverages. One outcome really is superior to the other. The illusion is, however, that two alternatives are never on the table at the same time. Good logic would have dictated that the councilman make a motion to spend $2.5 million dollars each year (the projected saving from water fluoridation) to get children to drink less soda.

When dentists buy supplies or patients select treatments, they compare desirable features. But the choice can only be among the various actual available bundles of features on offer. The fact that A costs more than the rest or will fail in 20 years is completely beside the point if *all-things-considered* A beats the other choices. There should be no red herring among the treatment options given to patients. ■

Brands and Independent Contractors

The nub:

1. There is a secondary market for professional ethics.

2. Ethics, as a cost of doing business, can be subcontracted.

3. Laws can be written to shift and disguise ethical risk.

Brands have value. That is certainly so for dentistry, where there are 120 practices with fictitious business names in San Francisco. That is part of the idea behind "corporate" dental practices.

The modern corporate business structure is a marvel because it permits segmentation and separate ownership of various aspects of the customer experience. The most successful limited liability corporations own the controlling and most profitable aspects of the enterprise and sell off the rest to independent contractors.

Ethics is one of those business assets or liabilities that can be spun off to maximize profit. Responsibility for fixing mistakes can be sold to others as easily as offering extended warranties or subcontracting with other outfits that are willing to buy one's boo-boos under their name. Companies can actually sell their ethical liabilities. Read the fine print.

The current masters are in Big Pharma. Consider "pay to delay" drug marketing settlements. A large firm faces revenue losses as its patent is about to expire and a startup readies to introduce a generic alternative. The business with a brand threatens a costly legal action, which has little chance of prevailing in court but would consume most of the small firm's resources and some taxpayers' funding of our justice system. Constraint of trade is dodged by reaching a court settlement where the generic manufacturer agrees to delay introduction of the competitive product for a period, say seven years, in exchange for several millions in cash payments from the larger firm each year. Both companies and their lawyers come out ahead, but at the expense of the public.

Specific case: The pharmaceutical company Aventis was making little from an anti-inflammatory orphan drug called Acthar, charging only $50 per vile. Protecting its brand image, it was afraid to raise prices out of fear of acquiring a reputation for price gouging. Aventis slithered out from under this ethical limitation by selling the patent to Questcor, evidently an outfit with no reputation to protect, for a nominal $100,000 plus a percentage on all future sales. A single dose of Acthar now costs $28,000. Aventis sold its ethical responsibility and got another company to do its dirty work.

Here is another trick where a company with a brand uses an entity with a weak reputation to extract money from the public. Insurance companies derive income from copayments on expensive brand-name drugs that they cannot get from the less expensive generics. Some manufacturers now offer to reimburse patients the copayment for continuing to buy their brand-name pills. Customers come out ahead. Manufacturers have to pay the insurance company a few bucks, but they are able to retain the much larger profit margin while using the insurance company to collect from employers and the government that underwrite the insurance contracts. Could happen in dentistry. ■

The nub:

1. The multiple roles we play each come with slightly different ethical scripts.

2. We can be primed to favor one way of behaving over others.

3. Expect others to act ethically and make it obvious.

Ethical Priming

Imagine a little research project where subjects are asked to complete a series of puzzles, such as finding patterns of numbers that add up to nine. A small monetary reward is given based on how many patterns can be found. Some participants self-score and others have their sheets checked by clerks.

But, drat, those social psychologists. They rummage in the trashcan and retrieve the coded answer sheets for the self-scorers. You guessed it: Many people in the "no check" conditions give themselves a little boost. The term popular for modest self-dealing is "personal fudge." It is virtually universal that we can think up reasons to privately balance the books of life.

Now, we add a third factor to our research design. Just before solving the puzzles, some of the subjects are asked to recall their favorite songs from when they were in high school. Others are asked to recall as many as possible of the Ten Commandments. The research proves two things: Virtually no one knows more than a few of the commandments and some mistakenly quote Ben Franklin or Shakespeare. The other finding is that regardless of how many of the moral precepts can be recalled, just thinking about them virtually wipes out the fudge.

This is called ethical priming. Being asked to assume a moral perspective makes people more ethical.

All of us have multiple moral self-images. We are members of peer review committees and colleagues practicing in the same specialty, commentators on civil society and voters, dentists and businesspersons. These roles have largely overlapping expectations, such as "appropriate" honesty and fairness. We seem to walk around with a little notebook of fundamental ethical expectations with slightly different lists on different pages. Sometimes we act on the scripts from one page and justify our actions from a different page.

So here is a natural question: Can ethical roles be primed? The research done so far is optimistic. In a typical study, ethical dilemmas such as use of expensive medical resources or informed consent versus performance quotas were presented to Army medics. Sometimes the medics were asked to present in uniform and were briefed by commanding officers in rooms with military insignia. Other times, they reported in scrubs with medical equipment present and were briefed by physicians. The same script was read in each situation and the same sorts of ethical dilemmas were considered.

The medics matched the moral perspective to the context. We are sensitive to cues in our environment that suggest the roles we are expected to play.

Consider the priming that takes place at C.E. courses, in our journals and other professional literature and at organized dentistry meetings. Which page in our book of scripts about right and wrong are we priming there? Much of ethics depends on which of our self-images show up. ■

Moral Decoys

I have a killer business plan, and I am looking for a few special people with the talent and vision to seize the opportunity. There is a crying and growing need for images demonstrating the damage that can be done by greedy, bureaucratic and misguided liberals and pseudo-scientists. My company would rent out victims to inform the public and embarrass the meddlers. The firm would be called Moral Decoys.

Of course, such firms already exist. They are a multibillion-dollar industry, mostly centered on public relations, lobbying and legal outfits. The correct technical name is a "front." The strategy is straightforward: Scare the public to prevent rule-makers from imposing unfavorable restrictions.

In the 1970s, proposed regulation of chlorofluorocarbons used in refrigeration was delayed and weakened by the Alliance for Responsible CFC Policy. On the outside, this was small manufacturers of air conditioning units and a group of citizen scientists working for the public good. Actually, it was a coalition of a few large chemical companies and was managed by a public relations firm. Early recycling legislation was opposed because it would put mom-and-pop operations out of business and create toxic pest hazards. Fluoride causes cancer. The Affordable Care Act was supposed to increase unemployment and tip the balance away from full-time to part-time work. The opposite has in fact been the case. The grandest of the moral decoys has been "shareholder interests." First noticed in the 1980s, CEOs have made it an all-purpose justification for short-term profit above all other considerations.

My business of renting out moral decoys will be based on two ethical pillars. First, actions are always undertaken for the benefit of others. One's own advantage will be held in strictest confidence. Second, ethical focus will be on specific individual cases. Statistics and overall impact are out of bounds.

If I could remember the individual's name, I would put him on the board of Moral Decoys. He was pretty famous back in the day when full-mouth cosmic reconstructions were going to bring dentistry to the stature it deserved. He was invited to give a talk on professional ethics to students at our dental school. He mostly showed his work, and there was no doubt that it was drop-dead gorgeous. He also made a point that insurance companies and uppity hygienists were literally bankrupting dentists, especially those losers who were trying to get by doing amalgams and prevention. A good 40 minutes into the presentation, he announced that he could summarize all of dental ethics on a single slide. It was a picture of two small children on wild animal skin rugs with large Harley-Davidsons in the background. He said, "I put my family first." ■

The nub:

1. One's own moral motives can be protected from scrutiny by claiming to be protecting others' interests.

2. The best dodge against moral responsibility is to avoid becoming a data point in general statistics.

3. Moral decoys are available for rent.

Looking the Other Way

The teenager killed her parents and then threw herself on the mercy of the courts because she was an orphan. Yes, in fact, ax murder Lizzy Borden was acquitted. Naturally, we want to think the best of ourselves and of others. It is generally agreed that winking at ethical violations will damage the profession. But the line of folks waiting to carry through with the "or else" part of the social contract is very short.

Holding others accountable can be both overdone and underdone. The dividing line is somewhere in the vicinity of whether we are doing it because it "makes us feel good" or because it protects innocent third parties who would be damaged by letting the bad practice continue. If we know that the rules and penalties are only pretend, we will all pretend to follow them. Reneging on enforcement for ethical violations can be both laudable clemency and questionable dodging of responsibility.

We cannot choose to play only the happy role. "People should just do what is right" is the wimpiest of false ethics imaginable. Righteous indignation is not much of a strategy either.

We get as much morality as we can afford. The problem is that the benefit of ethical behavior is to society generally, while the cost is to specific individuals or groups. We often seek to pass the cost of punishment on to others. The hangman of old wore a mask and was excluded from society.

Individuals can actually flitch personal prestige by short-circuiting punishment. In every culture, granting clemency is a sign of high social status. Only the governor can commute the death sentence. When we say, "I am letting it go this time," we elevate our own status. In surveys of cheating in colleges, the most common response to detected cheating is for faculty members to "deal with the problem on a personal and individual basis."

In addition to wanting to be judge and jury by personally dispensing mercy, we like to be legislators as well. When we selectively wink at bad acting, we are changing the rules. It is perfectly appropriate in a democracy to work to change the rules, say the laws requiring reporting of suspected child abuse. It is not appropriate to ignore the rules and expect to be exempt from the consequences. Finally, society is lousy at matching corrective action to unwanted behavior. Extreme forms of punishment have no more effect on behavior than do barely effective ones. One of my favorite cartoons shows the hangman placing a noose on the criminal's head and saying, "I hope this teaches you a lesson." On the other side, penalties that society is not willing to enforce are useless personal image building. ■

The nub:

1. In ethics, don't expect to get anything you are not willing to pay for.

2. Would you want to live in a world where "nobody" stood up for what is right?

3. Be on guard for private justice when public justice is ignored.

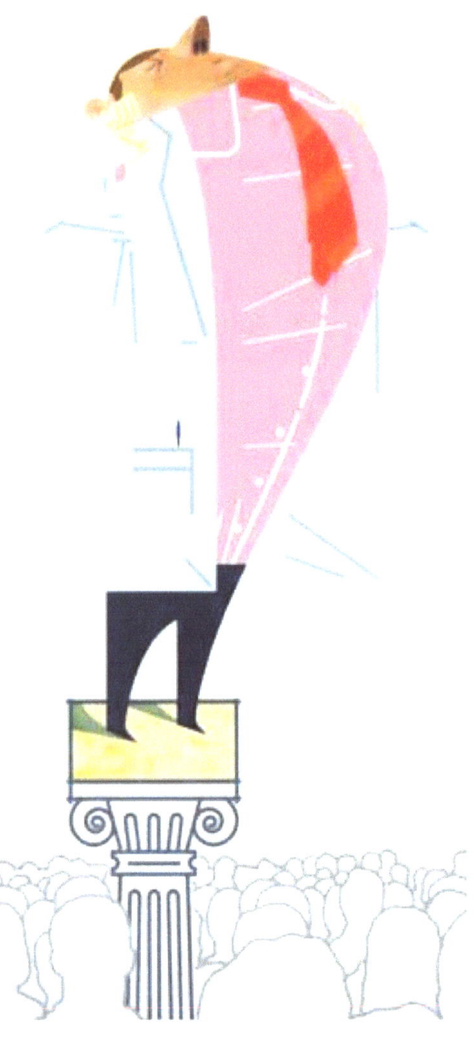

The nub:

1. Power can be a substitute for ethics.

2. We may have had enough of soapbox ethics.

3. Those who are most likely to bring ethics to dentistry are not dentists.

Power Ethics

Many journals are devoted to practical professional ethics. By rough count, there are 11 in bioethics, nine in medicine, six in business, three each in law, nursing and education and others in fields such as media, sports and the military. But there are none in dentistry, except for the recently introduced *Journal of Dental Ethics* published in India.

Several of the leading journals in dentistry offer regular columns. But much of what we write is editorial in nature and sometimes takes the form of scolding "others" by innuendo. To the best of my knowledge, there is no dental ethicist employed full time in a dental school, let alone several of them who could build an academic discipline.

Dentistry is unique among the professions in not having a cumulative scholarly base in ethics. Perhaps that is because dentists are just that much more ethical than are other professionals. Maybe it works fine to "borrow" the foundations for ethics from others. A case might be made that we pass ethics effectively to young practitioners in an informal way.

An alternative suggests itself in a recent article in a business ethics journal. It could be that there are "ethics substitutes."

Individuals in the study were given an ethical dilemma to solve as a group exercise. The outcome factors were how certain the decision-makers felt that they were doing the right thing and how much they used input from their colleagues. The researchers were interested in the relationship between power and ethics. They manipulated power by giving subjects a quiz to measure management, not ethical, skill.

Subjects who thought of themselves as powerful were less likely to consider the views of others involved in an ethical dilemma and were more confident in their choices. But that was bogus because the experimenters lied and randomly told half of the subjects the test showed them to be skilled and powerful while the others were not.

Dentists are high-power folks. Neither patients nor staff nor anyone else second-guesses the decisions, including ethical ones, made by dentists in their offices. They define ethics in the world where they live. This is in contrast to all the other professions that have their own dental ethics journals. Everywhere else, there are checks and balances as part of the practice routine. Medicine is hospital based, and business and law are played out in the give and take between equals.

If I am right in this analysis, we may begin to see some journals in dental ethics. The most powerful forces dentists interact with are their peers — including fellow dentists who may see things differently and owners, payers and regulators. Interacting with powerful others requires well thought-out justifications, and we need a team of qualified individuals working together in a cumulative fashion to do that work. ■

Shifting the Blame

The nub:

1. It is human nature to seek explanations for "unfortunate events" in ways that protect our personal image.
2. We overreact to negative events.
3. We place blame as far from ourselves as is plausible.

Over a period of 59 days beginning in February 1991, four children died and nine others sustained major injuries under suspicious circumstances on a single ward of a hospital in the United Kingdom. It was determined that a nurse, Beverley Allitt, administered lethal doses of insulin and used other means in her attacks. She is serving multiple life sentences.

Not quite the end of the story of course — there is the matter of fixing blame. A commission was created about two years later to inquire into the matter. This is human nature, as can be confirmed by watching the 6 o'clock news and waiting for the usual "No motive has yet been determined" and "Those responsible have not been identified." We need to finger the bad guys.

The Allitt inquiry considered testimony from 105 individuals, primarily other health care professionals on the ward where the tragedies occurred and administrators in the hospital. Although the complaint ultimately leading to criminal investigation came from a physician, most of the medical staff reported having been aware previously of the abnormal trends. No probing or reporting took place because it was "contrary to the ethics of professionals to engage in this sort of behavior." The hospital administration excused itself on principled generalizations: "It had always maintained the highest professional standards." At the same time, it was critical of the government for imposing onerous safety regulations and for underfunding health care generally. In the end, the heaviest criticism was reserved for administrators at one of the nursing programs Beverley Allitt attended for a brief time. Some records were discovered showing that she had exhibited "unusual behavior" while a student and did not respond well to offered help.

Humans process positive and negative information differently. Good news is largely taken for granted. Unwelcome discoveries are exaggerated in one of two ways. We may "catastrophize" and react righteously until we satisfy ourselves that those who are to blame are dealt with justly. The oppose extreme is about as likely — we cover the information in an "oh, no" blanket, discrediting the source or doubting that the event actually took place.

No one likes to see the garbage pile up on his or her doorstep. If we are powerful or clever enough, we will make certain that it is moved. Health care professionals had the best view of the Allitt mess. They were also the most facile at not seeing the problem and then moving it once pointed out. The Allitt report concluding that blame lay predominantly with a part-time education program is understandable but not useful. Those closest to bad behavior, best trained to identify it and in positions to take direct action have the greatest responsibility. If all health care trainees who exhibited "unusual behavior" should be barred from the professions, there would not be enough healing. ■

Do We Need a New Definition of Dentistry?

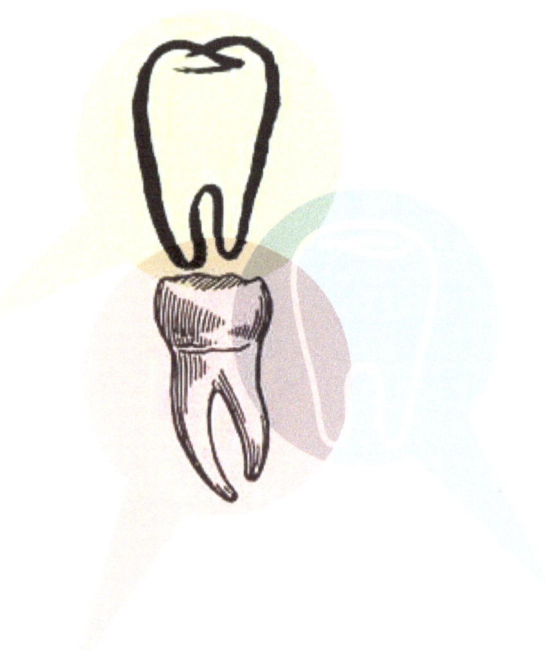

The nub:

1. Dentistry and oral health are not the same thing.

2. Opportunity without responsibility is a dangerous position to defend.

3. Larger scope necessitates decreased independence.

Every Saturday in America thousands of men buy three-eighth-inch drill bits. No one really wants a three-eighth-inch drill bit. Those who can help it avoid buying more than one. What we want is three-eighth-inch holes. The distinction is important. Customers want benefits, not features. Patients want oral health, not dentistry.

The American Dental Association recently proposed a definition of oral health as "a functional, structural, aesthetic, physiologic and psychosocial state of well-being [which] is essential to an individual's general health and quality of life." The FDI World Dental Federation has just developed a definition as well: "Oral health is multifaceted and includes the ability to speak, smile, smell, taste, touch, chew, swallow and convey a range of emotions through facial expressions with confidence and without pain, discomfort and disease of the craniofacial complex."

There is much to like in these definitions. They focus on the patient; they speak to a richer life for everyone.

The expanded ADA and FDI definitions represent both an opportunity and a liability. CBCT images open the prospect for dentists to treat obstructive sleep apnea, but they also place practitioners at legal risk for failing to diagnose oral cancers appearing in these images. Are dentists really responsible for patients' "total well-being," including "the ability to speak, smile, smell, taste, touch, chew, swallow and convey a range of emotions?" This seems to suggest the need for more training and collaboration with other professions. Wider scope means more responsibility.

But there is also danger in steering too close to the other side of the issue. Certainly dentists would not want to claim exclusivity for the new oral health outcomes being envisioned. Otolaryngologists, plastic surgeons, speech pathologists, psychologists, social workers and therapists of all types all have much to contribute to patients' total well-being. At the least, involving dentists in "functional, structural, aesthetic, physiologic and psychosocial states" of patients will require collaborative working relationships with a very large number of sister professionals. At the worst, we can expect turf wars.

Further, dentists may not want to assume complete responsibility even for traditional oral health care outcomes. Patients engage in inadequate home care, spotty follow up and damaging habits. Patients refuse optimal treatment plans and insurance companies may not pay for them. How can a dentist be held accountable for less than optimal oral health outcomes under such circumstances?

There is a balance between opportunity and responsibility and between proper action and outcomes. ■

Got Principles?

It is usually said that professions such as lawyers, ministers and doctors are more deserving of respect and trust than are beauticians, dog walkers and city planners because they have codes of ethics based on principles. Principles are general guides to behavior. There are dozens and dozens of these, from integrity to helping others, to "first do no harm," to confidentiality, to loyalty. Anyone who cannot find a principle to support his or her action is not trying very hard. And a few minutes on the web will show that virtually every group, including pro wrestlers and real estate agents now have codes of ethics based on principles.

Trade groups have always been more interested in ethics as principles than have philosophers. Philosophers avoid principles for a couple of reasons.

First, principles suggest what is right to do, but there is a lot of wobble in the system. They are "prima facie" rules, which is just a fancy way of saying "this is a controlling factor unless there are other more controlling factors." If there is no reason why a dentist should not treat mostly patients on welfare (on some principle such as putting patients' interests first), the dentist is compelled to do so.

Second, it is absolutely impossible to know when one has found the master moral principle. There is no true north on the moral compass. It is well known that multiple principles conflict. When that happens, professionals are supposed to make a "balanced" decision. There is no "balance" principle and the lead one could vary from person to person causing moral relativism.

Fifty years ago, my college roommate told a stale joke over dinner. He had just been tapped for Phi Beta Kappa and I wanted to know what somebody majoring in topology did. Here is what he said: A slice of bread can always (regardless of shape) be cut so that the two halves are identical in surface area. (You can see right away that this is about fairness.) Now a piece of ham can be added and a cut can still be made that guarantees parity. A third ingredient, perhaps mayo, makes it very difficult but justice can still be served. The fourth plane, always mustard in the story, is the deal breaker. There is no way a plane can be guaranteed to bisect four superimposed planes. Yeah, the punch line is, "Topologists have proven that you can't always cut the mustard."

It turns out that this impossibility theorem has been proven mathematically. There is no way we can be sure we have achieved a stable ethical when using all five of the traditional principles of patient respect, beneficence, nonmaleficence, justice and veracity. Even four will be impossible. ■

The nub:

1. If one wants to have justifications for any desired action, a very long list of principles is useful.

2. If one wants to have clear moral guidance, the set of principles should never be more than three.

3. Moving the principles around to suit the situation looks a lot like cheating.

Caring Enough to Criticize

The nub:

1. Honest peer criticism benefits the group as a whole.

2. Criticism only works in caring communities.

3. Start worrying when criticism from friends stops.

I played football in high school. Strictly second string. I did not mind because my senior year we went to the state championships and I got to square off against all-state tight end Rob Haskins four days a week. Our coach was named Spike Hilstrom. He was a bullet-shaped, baby-faced former lineman for one of the state colleges.

Playing in the line is about center of balance, heads up, wide stance and owning as much space as possible. One of Spike's drills involved two linemen, face to face, north to south, with a two-by-four board running north to south between our legs. This taught a wide stance. It was fatal to bring your feet directly under you as one would naturally do. The cleats would slide on the board and down you went. I was no match for Haskins and remember much time on my face with Spike Hilstrom yelling at me. Did I tell you he had an unnaturally annoying voice?

After one session, Coach called me aside and said, "Chambers, I can tell that you do not like me yelling at you." [silence] "I'll tell you why I bother to yell at you. It's because I respect you and I want to see you do better." [silence] "Chambers, you should start to worry when I stop yelling. That means I have stopped caring."

I have been reading the disciplinary reports of the California Dental Board. I am saddened at the level of bad dentistry and personal stupidity of some dentists. I am heartened that patients, office staff and investigators in the attorney general's office are speaking up about it.

In the Common Good Game used in research, players have an opportunity to increase their payoff (money) by cooperating. This is much like the profession's reputation in dentistry. The smart move for *individuals* is to let others invest and reap the common benefits without becoming involved. The smart move for the *group* is for everyone to invest and share in the common reward.

Under normal circumstances, initial modest investments dry up as players notice that their colleagues are free riding. Everyone bends a little as the cheaters prosper. But when players are allowed to criticize their neighbors, free riding stops and *everyone* does better.

It is easy but wrong to believe human nature is good just because bad acting is not commented on or that undesirable behavior will improve if ignored. The most recent research does clarify, however, that criticizing the deviously selfish does not always work. In groups low on trust or those who see others as competitors, criticism does not lead to improvements.

Spike was right. He cared enough to make me a contributor on the state championship team. Perhaps he did not need to care in public at 90 decibels, but I am glad he cared. ■

Misunderstanding Generational Differences

The nub:

1. Those in charge will find it futile to ask why the rising generation is uninterested in playing the old game.

2. Group behavior today is based on local interactions.

3. Ten years ago we should have been worrying about membership; today we should try to understand what it means to be a dentist.

Before we had fake news, there was an urban legend that beginning dentists were unethical because of their heavy educational debt. There are no published studies supporting this claim. The average age for disciplined physician and dentist licenses in California is in the mid-50s. Cheating in dental schools has been about 70 percent recently, compared with the low 90 percent range in the 1980s. A research paper published in this journal in 2002 found no connection between debt and "nontraditional treatment plans." Educational debt plus interest have risen by an average of $5,800 each year since 1985. But for most of this period total debt was a constant three-quarters of general practitioners' net income for a single year. What changed in about 2005 when the rumors linking educational debt and unethical practice began to surface was that established dentists' earnings went flat.

The times change for everyone. All of dentistry is becoming more commercial, privileging ICD codes over care, membership in organized dentistry is declining at 1 percent per year while fictitious business names proliferate, dentists say they create smiles rather than health, and more and more they look to vendors rather than colleagues for values. Ethics is too often defined as coming close enough to minimal compliance with the law. The personalities of generations are a result of how they react to the continual changes in society.

Today, the young ones are characterized as "selfish," "now oriented," "FOMO — fear of missing out," "team oriented" and participating in the social cause de jour. I recall when baby boomers were labeled "entitled," "smug," "driven" and "expecting to live (practice and retain control) forever." Often the older generation is locked into fighting the wars of 30 years ago, while the new generation sees emerging challenges.

Generation X grew up playing *The Legend of Zelda*. It is grounded in the classic myth of a solo hero saving the princess in distress by overcoming obstacles to acquire "powers" and move to new levels. Baby boomer parents approved of the mission. After all, they were moving through the chairs in organized dentistry and building secure futures "for their families." What was objectionable was the "virtual" nature of Gen-Xers' participation. Success was possible without the blessing of authority.

Millennials cut their teeth on *SimCity*. This is a massively multiplayer online game, where a huge virtual community interacts in real time to build worlds that are individually satisfying. The goal is personally defined, the rules are few and outcomes are determined by what one does in the context of what others are doing. Unenforced rules are just PR slogans. Communities emerge based on local interactions and they change shape quickly. That sure puts a stick in the spokes of large organizations' top-down strategic planning. ■

Which Is Worse for Dentistry: Markets or Regulation?

The nub:

1. Markets are a fair means of exchanging known quantities – price is known by patients, quality of care is not.

2. Regulation primarily benefits organized special interest groups.

3. It is an open question whether professionalism can survive the changing forces of the market and regulation.

During the past decade as dentistry has become more about appearance and cost, dentists' incomes have stagnated and in some cases declined. If dentistry loses its unique status as a regulated professional monopoly, there is no certainty that either the free market or regulation will protect it.

Here is the logic regarding markets. Even in the best of worlds, patients will never know enough about when to seek care or how to choose the best available options. Information asymmetry is part of the arrangement and it is cost-ineffective to attempt to entirely remove that barrier.

Better quality care is necessarily more expensive. Put in negative terms, someone can always do it cheaper and worse. Thus there will always be a quality/price gap where patients are unable to recognize the whole value they receive for higher cost. Such gaps are not evident when buying a car or a meal in a restaurant because the consumer can see pretty much all of the benefit. In oral health, quality is latent. Great skill may be needed in case unanticipated complications arise and the best care reduces or eliminates the signals of quality patients can judge for themselves.

The market is a blunt instrument for reducing the quality/price gap. We cannot count on advertising to correct information asymmetries. Because we cannot adequately evaluate quality, the gap will tend to be closed by offering lower quality at lower prices. We have home bleaching and home orthodontics. Corporate models of delivery emphasize volume and standardized treatment plans.

The market aspect of dentistry is controlled by the Department of Consumer Affairs, not the profession. Licenses are granted to construction firms, cosmetologists, social workers, dentists and others to function as market entities. The standard is low on the grounds that more services are better for the public. A minimal standard is set for safety and customers are allowed to select the level of quality they can discern and afford.

The alternative is regulation — a mixed blessing. It is expensive, sometimes produces unexpected or even paradoxical results and is intended to benefit one group at the expense of another. Dentistry, as a well-organized special interest group, has enjoyed monopoly status and consistently raised the minimal standard of care. Monopolistic regulation focuses on the high end of the quality/price gap, holding up both and denying access to care for many.

Historically, dentistry has balanced the market and regulatory mechanisms quite successfully. This has been possible because dentistry has been organized and the public has not. These conditions are changing. Many in the profession have started selling smiles instead of health, and that in dollar-denominated terms. New, well-organized interest groups are pushing for regulatory adjustments at exactly the time when membership in organized dentistry is dropping. ■

The Ethics Help Desk

The nub:

1. Morality is a habit, built over a lifetime.
2. The best time to work on morality is now.
3. Needing ethics often signals a failure of moral identity.

Many people use the terms "morals" and "ethics" interchangeably. I do not. Morals is our behavior, especially our habits, which affect others for good or not. Ethics is what we say about it. Morality is a life-time pattern of conduct, mostly evident in not taking advantage of others. When people start talking ethics, I fear they are looking to justify something they recognize as questionable. Sometimes ethics talk is about "somebody else" doing something the speaker disapproves of.

There are some really wonderful people who cannot spell nonmaleficence or explain the difference between the CDA Code of Ethics and the ADA Code of Professional Conduct positions on justifiable criticism.

The *Mabinogeon* is an ancient Welsh collection of tales. There is a useful one in the story of Culhwch and Olwen. King Arthur met a spirit, rather small and indifferent in form. As the spirit approached, it gradually resembled an incompletely formed man — and it challenged King Arthur to wrestle. The king declined, disdaining the effort and realizing that he would gain little credit for defeating such an inconsiderable character. Repeated challenges were put aside as the creature grew in size. Eventually, Arthur was forced to engage and only barely succeeded in overcoming the spirit. Its Welsh name means "half man;" it is also translated as "habit."

Morality is a habit, laid down in small pieces over a lifetime. Rarely does it rise to the level of consciousness. It is just part of our identity. It controls the way we see the world. And most of us are not morally deficient, we are morally blind. We have created a world that is comfortable to live in and which distances us from the inconvenience of others. Habits are self-protective.

Moral crises are extremely rare. We have constructed the world so as to avoid them. A common response when we might be thought to be off base is to fabricate a justification for this being a special case. Facility with ethical principles helps; we consult the ethical help desk. But perhaps, like King Arthur, this is a signal that we have waited too long.

"Do I really have to . . .?" The likelihood of doing an online search, reading several chapters in an ethics text or reflecting for a few hours on a moral decision is vanishingly small. The chances of getting advice at the help desk that leads to an ethical conversion is also tiny.

Amos Tversky, the lifetime collaborator of Nobel Laureate Danial Kahneman, held that the big decisions, such as who one falls in love with, one's school or first job and what equipment one buys, have a large element of chance in them. It is the small decisions made every day about margins, relating to patients, honest billing and being open to one's colleagues that define who we are. ■

Professional Blindness

The nub:

1. Poor moral eyesight is a larger problem than ethical muscle cramps.

2. Belonging to a group that strongly professes ethical standards can be detrimental to acting morally.

3. Immorality that is not noticed is not corrected.

Here's a surefire conversation nonstarter, "Let's talk about some of the unethical things we have been doing recently." On the other hand, we often do enjoy a few minutes topping each other with reports of the corruption, cheating, misrepresentation and motivated political shenanigans of those not present. Funny thing about immorality — the farther it is from us, the more certain we are that it is going on.

In 1964, a woman named Kitty Genovese was abused, beaten and eventually murdered on the streets of Queens in New York City. Parts of the event, which lasted about half an hour, were witnessed by a confirmed 38 people. None of them took any initiative to stop the tragedy. None of them phoned the police.

Thanks to a series of ingenious experiments, we now know some useful things about moral blindness. In a typical study, research subjects complete a questionnaire (which really has nothing to do with the study) while being interrupted during this process with an "emergency" that would normally reframe the situation so that a civil response is expected. In one study, smoke was piped into the ventilation panel in the room where the questionnaire was being completed. In another, a female research assistant left the room and a loud noise was heard as though she had been hit or taken a fall. There was also a variation where an epileptic attack was simulated in the hall just outside the door. The question was whether the subject would stop doing the survey and take helpful action.

The answer is generally yes. In the three conditions described, the moral response of interrupting the routine and offering help was taken by 75 percent, 70 percent and 85 percent of the subjects when alone. But here is the twist. If there were three research subjects in the room, the probability that any of them would intervene in the first case (smoke) dropped to 38 percent. When there were two subjects in the case of the simulated fall, only 40 percent responded. When there were five subjects who heard the mock epileptic attack, only 40 percent responded. When subjects were paired with confederates who were instructed to ignore the moral call, the proportion of responsive subjects dwindled to the 10 percent range.

The lesson is that the more plausible it is to assume that others will do the right thing, the less likely we are to do it ourselves. Being part of a profession, especially one that takes a bold public stance favoring ethics, may actually impede seeing moral issues or acting to correct them. Patients (individuals who do not subscribe to a professional ethical code) are more likely to bring an action against a dentist for malpractice than are staff members, and they are more likely to initiate actions than are professional colleagues. ■

Alt-Logic

The nub:

1. All facts are alt-facts; it is the interpretation that matters.

2. If dentistry were reducible to objective reality, staff or computers would replace dentists.

3. Agreement with others is a matter of perspective; unless we can see as others do, we are pretty certain to disagree.

Frankly, I have had enough of alt-truths. In the end, the facts are not determinative: It is the interpretation that counts. Most of us know where to get the facts we want, conveniently packaged in our favorite interpretations. And as for the other guy's supposed facts, here are some convenient defenses: "It might be premature to comment," "probability is not certainty," "the sample size is too small" and "beware of overgeneralizing."

Information is a combination of the facts and the assumptions we make about what they would mean for us if true. When we witness a car accident or get an exposure, we say "Oh, no." It is instinct to deny unwanted facts. The evaluation is instantaneous as though we were shielding ourselves from something we do not acknowledge as the case.

If we don't like the facts, we can make adjustments for the source. It is easy enough to say the radiograph is not diagnostic. Insurance will not cover this. Dentists do not choose a staff member or associate exclusively on the information about the candidate or they would all be after the same ones. Dentists typically diagnose the condition of a tooth by combining what they see with their years of clinical wisdom regarding "these kinds of teeth." It is human nature to combine real, particular data with information about cases of a general nature. The sophisticated name for this is evidence-based dentistry.

The critical question is how much weight should be placed on the facts and how much on generalizations about where the facts came from and what they mean. Typically, decisions that are based on an honest combination of facts and their sources are better than decisions that undervalue either. There are formal techniques for this.

So it may be correct to say "beware of generalizations," but it is incorrect to say we can get rid of them. Better by far to say "be aware of generalizations." It is unethical to use logic that misleads others by protecting our generalizations at the expense of inconvenient facts. What makes this an ethical matter is picking only the facts we want or distorting them to match our generalizations. The patient who declines the obvious best health options does so either because he or she has not been given full informed consent or because the common facts are placed in different contexts. Change the context rather than the facts. A colleague who engages in what you may consider to be questionable treatment may have diagnosed the case exactly as you have. What is needed before judgment is comparing the contexts. ■

All in the Family

Throughout history, the established generation has insisted on its privilege of grumbling about the younger generation disrespecting the norms of their elders. Those who will inherit the future have insisted on their privilege of grumbling about how conditions are changing and the old norms need a dustup. Why should it be any different today in dentistry?

Before we had fake news, there was an urban legend that beginning dentists were unethical because of their heavy educational debt. There are no published studies that confirm this claim. The average age for disciplined licenses for physicians and dentists in California is in the mid-50s. A research paper published in this journal in 2002 found no connection between debt and "nontraditional treatment plans." Educational debt plus interest have risen by an average of $5,800 each year since 1985. But during the first two-thirds of this period, the debt was a constant three-quarters of general practitioners' net incomes for a single year, which were rising at almost double inflation. What changed in about 2005 when the rumors linking educational debt and unethical practice began to surface was that dentists' earnings went flat.

Hot sellers in the bookstores these days are titles advising managers how to deal with younger workers. Tellingly, there are few books going the other way, presumably because millennials get their information from other sources. The young ones are characterized as "selfish," "now oriented," "FOMO — fear of missing out," "team oriented" and participating in the social cause du jour. I recall when baby boomers were labeled "entitled," "smug," "driven" and "expecting to live (practice and retain control) forever." Both characterizations have sufficient truth, and both are inadequate because they assume that intergenerational differences are a function only of a collective personality. Groups, including generations, respond based on where they stand relative to changing conditions and what others like them are doing.

Gen Xers grew up playing The Legend of Zelda, a video game grounded in the classic myth of a solo hero saving the princess in distress by overcoming obstacles to acquire "powers" and move to new levels. Baby-boomer parents approved of the mission. After all, they were moving through the chairs in organized dentistry and building secure futures "for their families." What was objectionable was the virtual nature of the Gen Xer's participation. Success was possible without the blessing of authority.

Millennials cut their teeth on SimCity. Players in this massively multiplayer online game interact in real time to build worlds that are individually satisfying. The goal is personally defined, the rules are few and outcomes are determined by what one does in the context of what others are doing. Unenforced rules are just PR slogans. Communities emerge based on local interactions and they change shape quickly. That sure puts a stick in the spokes of large organizations' top-down strategic planning. ■

The nub:

1. Those in charge will find it futile to ask why the rising generation is uninterested in playing the old game.

2. Group behavior today is based on local interactions as power shifts to the masses.

3. Ten years ago we should have been worrying about membership; today we should try to understand what it means to be a dentist.

A Plague of Laws

Aristippus of Cyrene, an ancient Greek philosopher, said it would be easy to identify an ethical person: Look for the one who, when all intelligent laws are passed and enforced, would not change his behavior.

The politicians have misstated the problem: We do not have too much government; we have too many laws. The famous Italian economist Vilfredo Pareto, who invented the 80-20 rule, proposed that taxes should be entirely voluntary because it is patently obvious that the more we contribute to the common good, the more everyone gains. There has been some hesitancy on the concept, so legislators have been working to be more specific. Currently, Title 26 of the United States Code — our federal tax law — comes in 20 volumes, 16,845 pages and is available for purchase at $1,153, including shipping. There is still no good evidence that anyone has actually read it.

It has been observed by wise people such as Lao Tzu, a fifth century BCE Chinese philosopher, Edward Gibbon in his *The History of the Decline and Fall of the Roman Empire* and Jay Leno that the only certain consequence of more rules is a reliable increase in the number of rule breakers.

Laws come in two flavors. There are those that cannot be broken, such as gravity, greed and the impossibility of living to be 150. The other type is convention with penalties attached in hopes of redistributing benefits and costs. Regulations of dental practice are examples of selectively adjusting who benefits from and who pays for oral health.

Arguably the best known philosopher of the last century was John Rawls. In his masterpiece, *A Theory of Justice*, Rawls argued that Western liberalism depended on everyone having an opportunity to maximize his or her economic position. But there are two qualifications: Laws should not be created that (a) restrict social mobility and (b) no one should be allowed to benefit at the expense of others. A plague of laws comes from selectively tilting the playing field.

The Black Death of the 14th century is a fascinating example because it created capitalism as we know it. The 50 percent mortality rate in Europe wiped out the agricultural labor force. Wages started to rise, but were checked by laws fining landowners from paying more and forcing laborers to work and preventing them from moving.

The man-made laws could not hold back the natural laws of economics. We all find ways to work around inappropriate laws and regulations. The laws to preserve an ineffective system remained on the books but were ignored and creative work-arounds were found. The only place in Europe that was spared the plague was Russia, and serfdom remained the standard there for another 500 years.

Laws and regulations can be established to redistribute the goods and benefits in society, but they cannot reallocate human needs. ■

The nub:

1. Ethics cannot be legislated.
2. Attempts to do so often redistribute benefits to the powerful.
3. Natural law eventually corrects man-made law, after an appropriate period of hypocrisy.

The Greatest Fear of All

Snakes and spiders are often anxiety provoking and even debilitating. Urban legend has it that public speaking is the most widespread fear. Millennials tweet the abbreviation FOMO to reference "fear of missing out." As real as these are in specific situations, they are not the greatest fear because potentially problematic situations can be avoided.

The real fear must be a constant, inescapable threat that puts our very being or sense of identity at risk. And the biggie is fear of being wrong or FOBW. To live in society means constant exposure everywhere to others who instinctively are on the lookout for catching us off base.

The "wrong" treatment plan, a practice philosophy others disagree with, supporting the wrong candidate, being too adventuresome or too conservative about technology — somebody is bound to disagree. And this goes beyond an act or a statement: It is about our identity. It is fear of BEING wrong — the wrong sort of person. Antifluoridationists, amalgam-free dentists, absentee corporate owners, cosmetologists and young practitioners with high educational debt are not colleagues who, among their many virtues, also sometimes act and say things we would not. They are the wrong kind of people.

We push back against FOBW exactly because it is a threat to our identity.

The best protection against FOBW is to find a justification for our position and any plausible justification will do. All we really need is to convince ourselves that there is some reason for our being the way we are. We are quite skilled at this. In philosophy there is even a specialized subdiscipline devoted to this skill called casuistry.

Justifications are ad hoc, disposable and easy. There is no requirement that our justifications be consistent. In fact, the ADA Principles of Ethics states in the introduction that "principles can overlap each other as well as compete with each other for priority." Conspiracy theories are the general purpose, industrial-strength justification. Usually we pick one that works at the moment and that is sufficient.

Because the utility of justifications is self-protection, they are weak equipment for advancing the common good. In fact, they often block constructive discussion. Virtually no one is incapable of manufacturing an excuse against considering others' points of view. Flip back and forth between Fox and MSNBC to test this theory. Advocates on both sides of the abortion issue or government spending or live patients on one-shot initial licensure exams are fully justified. Evidence-based dentistry has had less effect on practice than its advocates had hoped, to some extent because we have not paid sufficient attention to the integration of the multiple valid justifications for the complex practice of dentistry.

FOBW causes deep pain. But pain has survival value in directing our responses toward safer behavior. Justifications are cheap, temporary placebos. ■

The nub:

1. The greatest fear of all is fear of being wrong.

2. The best defense against FOBW is self-justification and any justification will do.

3. Sometimes we are wrong and justification prevents learning.

It Is Better to Give

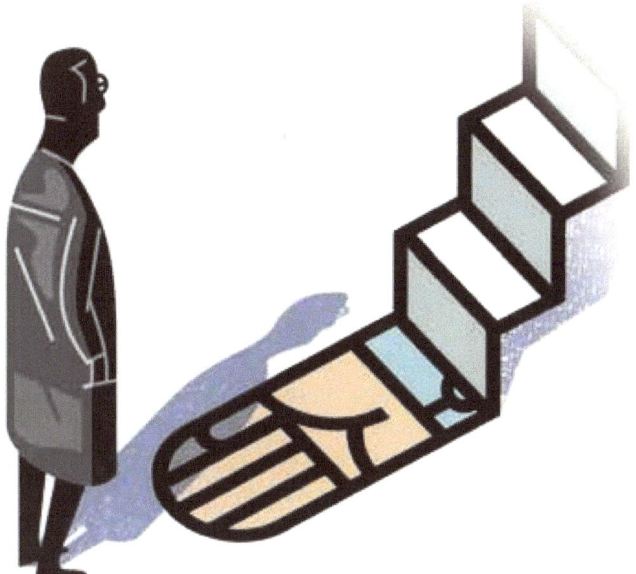

The nub:

1. Help, particularly unasked-for assistance, is often resented.

2. We all have our threshold for what we think is fair.

3. Pro bono work promotes good feelings about the underserved.

Here is a paradox: We often have more positive attitudes toward those we help than those who help us. This was a popular sentiment during the 18th century. In his autobiography, Benjamin Franklin said, "This is another instance of the truth of an old maxim I had learnt, which says, he that has once done you a kindness will be more ready to do you another, than he whom you yourself have obliged." His contemporary, the Scottish philosopher David Hume, expressed it this way: "We attach ourselves more by the services we perform than by those we receive."

We tend to discount our indebtedness to those who help us. We dislike being dependent.

In 2015, Americans spent roughly $118 billion on dental care. Let's imagine something very dramatic: Let's cap this at $47 billion, total, for all dentists. Dentists could perform as much dentistry as they felt that the public needed, but less than half of what was formerly paid for would be compensated.

Patients only pay about $40 of every $100 from their own pockets. About 45 percent comes from benefits programs (mistakenly called "insurance") and 15 percent from the government. Although external sources have allowed dentistry to be performed at a much higher level than it was about a half-century ago when the payment mix started to change, I know very few dentists who publically sing the praises of insurance or government. The general sentiment is to grouse, almost to the point of ingratitude.

I have mentioned the Ultimatum Game before. In the game, Player A is given a sum of money free, usually equivalent to a day's wages. For convenience we will say $100. Player A can share any amount up to $100 with Player B, a stranger who has no claim on the money. If Player B accepts the offer, the amount is split as agreed. If Player B declines the offer, neither A or B get anything. Both insurance and the income tax system come to mind as examples.

The Ultimatum Game has been played innumerable times in countries and social classes all over the world. Even in one-off exchanges, an offer of about $30 of the $100 is accepted while offers of less are usually rejected. The receiving party would rather have nothing than an amount he or she considers "unfair." Dentists often say things like this with regard to insurance or government-supported care, but most accept the offer. Presumably, current compensation arrangements meet the grumble threshold but are better than the deal threshold.

We are committed to advance the interests of those whom we help, not those who have given us a hand up. Ask any dentists who have volunteered at a CDA Cares event or a mission to an underdeveloped country. ■

Ethics of Practice Location

The nub:

1. Where one practices determines how one practices.

2. It is good business to segment the market, but it may not be good ethics.

3. The poor get less care and of poorer quality.

Practice location is perhaps the single largest ethical decision a dentist will ever make. It affects what patients expect and will accept, thus how one practices. The impact of that single decision is repeated day after day.

Wait a minute! Isn't where one lives a personal choice? Yes, but ethical choices are personal ones. Where we practice becomes part of our professional identity.

Surveys of graduating seniors have consistently revealed a small tendency to establish practices in one's own ethnic community. There are lifestyle issues that draw graduates to remote areas for the quality of small-town or outdoor living. One's spouse has a say.

But economic factors have a strong pull.

One can assuage anxieties about practicing on the least needy by volunteering. These are temporary, selective interventions — almost always in areas remote from one's own practice. There are dentists, and they deserve respect and credit, who prefer to give back in their own communities. There are some who actively work to extend the range of potential patients to include a broader range of their neighbors. Bravo for them, but we need more.

Practice location is not randomly distributed across California. If it were, the ratio of dentists to population would be similar across counties. Instead, there are more than 50 dentists per 50,000 population in Marin, Santa Clara, San Francisco and around Lake Tahoe. By contrast, there are six per 50,000 in Yuba County and none in Alpine.

I recently checked the median household incomes by ZIP code around the state. The average in 2015 was $61,818 per household. We would expect that dentists, on average, would practice in ZIP codes where the average was close to that figure. Instead, dentists concentrated in areas where the median household income was $79,094. That is a 28 percent step up in potential economic support for practitioners.

That in and of itself suggests that practice location might be an ethical issue. But if we look farther at how dentists practice, the concern grows. Some dentists have their licenses disciplined in California (about 50 per year). Some of this is because of life issues such as drugs or tax evasion. There are cases of failure to diagnose cancer or placing implants where they are unjustified. Dentists guilty of these infractions are likely to locate in upscale neighborhoods just like their colleagues do.

But there are many disciplined licenses resulting from overtreatment, overbilling and insurance fraud, failure to inform patients of their treatment options and patient abandonment. These dentists practice in communities where the median household income is 10 percent below the state average. That is certainly an ethical issue. ■

Disclosing Ethical Secrets

The nub:

1. The reputation of the profession matters just as the reputation of its members does.

2. It is a double ethical challenge to act based on what we know unless we have permission to know that sort of thing.

3. Ethical principles are sometimes used as an excuse to cover systemic ethical weakness.

The marketing folks tell us that "leaked secrets" is an inviting phrase and much more likely to prompt interest than the word "ethics." My point will be that there is even greater power in being able to suppress ethical secrets. It is one of the new ethical norms: "I know something that could help others, but I can't tell because I am so ethical."

A colleague sent me a CV to review as he was considering nominating this individual for fellowship in the American College of Dentists. On paper, this was a clear shot. But I happened to know a little background about the case because of a "need to know" relationship with the university. The possible candidate was under administrative sanction for violation of ethical standards. The university had screened my colleague and others from getting this information. What should I say?

The rationale for the secrecy was to protect the faculty member's reputation. Quite possibly the university was protecting itself as well from bad publicity and possible legal action. But a penalty that no one knows about has to be considered a strange one.

Ethicists debate these things: If you have been damaged (say, by praising someone who should not be praised) but are not aware that you have misled others, is it wrong? Yes, and the fault lies with the third party that has unnecessarily covered an ethical secret for its own advantage.

Disciplined licenses for dentists are public records and a quick check will show that the proportion of disciplinary actions in some states, such as California, is two or three times the rate in other states. It is not because California dentists are unethical. Phone conversations with responsible agents indicate that many states simply lack sufficient enforcement resources and others try to suppress information about inconvenient facts.

Several billboards appeared in 2016 in another state asking motorists to consider whether their dentist was honest. The phone number of the state association was displayed at the bottom of the message inviting drivers to phone and find out. This is a frightening use of innuendo. I know exactly what happened, but no one I talked with in the state or nationally seems to have any knowledge of this ethical secret.

There are two levels of ethical knowledge: What one knows and what one is allowed to know.

These are tough cases, but generally it works well to keep the secret when there is a potential for harm to others. If there is potential harm in keeping the secret, think about speaking up. If it is really a tight situation, confront the person or organization that is responsible for the gag order and challenge them to be ethical. ■

Ethical Equipoise

The nub:

1. In ethics, you get what you are willing to pay for.

2. Being critical of what others do is not ethics; it is smugness.

3. All situations that are *treated* the same way are ethically indifferent.

If ethics is valuable, we should expect to pay a little something for it. The ethics we get for free may not be the best quality. Value is a reflection of what we are prepared to do, not what we want.

Equipoise means being generally indifferent to any of the plausible alternatives in a situation. Some examples: The patient has no preference for full extractions and dentures or just pulling the one that hurts today; the practitioner says the same things in public about colleagues who do great work and those known to deliver gross or continuous faulty treatment; some see no need to belong to or participate in organized dentistry — "the profession will be the same with me or without me."

This does not mean that dentists are indifferent about outcomes. As a species, humans are exquisitely talented at forming preferences and having opinions. Have you noticed the polarization in America today? Few can watch a football game on television between two schools they have never heard of for more than five minutes without picking a favorite. No dentists can look in a patient's mouth without instantly "seeing" the treatability of the case.

The confusion comes in *correctly* recognizing that one has clear and consistent preferences among outcomes but *incorrectly* equating this with ethics. All the outcomes one is prepared to do nothing about are of equal ethical weight. Whether we are ethical depends on the choices we made, not on whether we like the results. After the outcomes are revealed, we cheer or hiss or grumble. Before the outcomes are revealed, any courses of action about which we are indifferent are considered to be in ethical equipoise.

Discount ethics is quite the thing these days. The basic idea is to spend as little as possible in hopes of still getting by. The cheapest form of discount ethics is to blame others or to say they should be doing things the way we want. Good bargains are also to be had by writing codes and advertising them. Enforcing them is avoided because it is expensive and drains the public-relations value of ethical posturing. A bargain is to be had and has been used by the dental trade by awarding publicized prizes for being ethical.

There is an old saw in business advising that every organization (or profession or individual) is perfectly designed to produce exactly the level of dysfunction it is willing to accept. The principle of ethical equipoise says that a profession achieves exactly the level of ethics it is willing to pay for. This is usually not the same as the level it thinks it is entitled to, wants, enshrines in codes or editorializes about. ■

Fibbing

The nub:

1. Fibbing is about who benefits from twisted truth, not whether truth is twisted.

2. It is always possible to concoct a backstory to justify a claim about what one needs to believe.

3. Fibbing is good for business but corrodes relationships.

Some wag said that the first casualty in war is truth. But fibbers will tell you dentistry is not war, so bending the truth is acceptable if it serves a purpose. That is flat-out false logic, but it is certainly not uncommon to hear people reason this way.

Why do any dentists sell treatment that is patently or even arguably not needed without disclosing alternatives? Why do they fail to mention a big overhang or incomplete endo they left in hopes that it might not cause a problem or, if it does cause a problem, they expect to negotiate proportional responsibility with the patient? Why are more and more dentists offering standardized treatment plans to mass markets? Why does the most recent Gallup poll of trust in the professions show dentists at the bottom of health care providers and neck and neck with police officers, with a 5 percent drop in public trust in the profession during the past six years?

We have had quite enough editorializing about why it is wrong to fib (with certain qualifications). We are getting tired of this "moralizing." We are now numb to fibbing and in danger of ceasing to care about it. Perhaps we have overlooked the opportunities opened by allowing multiple truths.

Telling the truth means saying only what one knows to be the case. Lying is saying things one knows not to be so. Fibbing means enhancing one's prospects by saying what it is hoped others will accept as being fact. This is a creative blending of misfocused facts and motivation.

Fibbing turns on believability not veracity. The fabulous fibber cares less about what is the case and more about whether others will accept a claim (or strategic silence) from which the fibber benefits. We all create worlds we prefer to believe in. Fibbers offer others believable alternatives that depend to some extent on perceived expertise and largely on fear and fantasy. Mendacity can be smoked out by fact-checking. Not so for fibbing. There the test is who benefits and who is harmed by accepting an offered version of reality.

Overtreatment is a fib because there will always be "evidence" or an "expert for hire" who confirms the need for the care while at the same time the patient loses and the dentist benefits from the motivated misstatement. It is just business and some justification can be found if needed.

Patients want to trust dentists, so they usually avoid looking too deeply into anything other than cost. As one patient said recently in a focus group, "If I think the dentist is overselling, overcharging or has even committed malpractice, I will simply walk away. They can always prove that they are right, even when it hurts the rest of us." ■

Training Wheels for Cheaters

Art Dugoni is the master at making it easy for people to contribute to the profession. But it isn't always through the big gift. Sometimes it is $100 from an alum whom we hadn't heard from in years. Art would smile and say, "Consider it a training gift."

Art is right. Kindness and charity are not events, they are processes. And exactly the same logic applies to moral decay. The surgeon in the Midwest who lost his license for grossly unsanitary office conditions did not commit one big ethical misstep — it was a habit built over a lifetime. Insurance companies catch and successfully prosecute fraud based on patterns of abuse. One bad claim, even if outrageous, often goes through or is challenged in a way that permits graceful retreat. The average age of both physicians and dentists in California who have their licenses disciplined is in the late 50s.

An endo file breaks. After some soul-searching and because the patient says nothing, the dentist overlooks the matter. Another instrument misbehaves; now it is understood that "this sort of thing happens." A dentist treats a patient until the family breadwinner is out of work and has no insurance. Soon a pattern emerges of aggressive treatment up to the insurance allowance and then protecting the economic interests of the office through formal discharge letters. A routine extraction turns out to be more difficult than anticipated. If one is motivated and makes the right sorts of inquires of friends or online, they can learn how to find the radiographs necessary for upcoding.

Some dentists or dental students hear about techniques for "educating" patients to accept levels of treatment they do not need and cannot afford, but most professionals say "not for me" to this sort of thing. Some have an opportunity to receive coaching in these doubtful practices in an associateship or other employment arrangement. But it requires a combination of bad examples, pressure situations, "successful" small experiments and repetition over time to form bad habits.

There is no reason to expect that it is any different going in the positive direction. A few admonitions from a respected leader in the profession or a couple of dilemma cases is not going to get the job done. Up or down depends mostly on what happens after the experimental behavior is tried.

There is a story that Bernie Madoff's outrageous misconduct was an accident that might have corrected itself. This nefarious career began with a single bad investment that he intended to cover with an accounting adjustment until the next ship came in. Unfortunately, the next ship was also a mishap. Worse yet, none of Madoff's friends offered help or asked for an explanation. Silence of his colleagues was part of the pattern. ■

The nub:

1. "The first time you cheat is difficult; after that it gets easier." – J. R. Ewing, *Dallas*

2. Big cheats all started as small ones.

3. Conscience is best built or dismantled in small steps.

The Moral Compass and the Moral Code

The nub:

1. More than a moral compass is needed to navigate the ethical landscape.

2. Compasses are unreliable except for the grossest distinctions.

3. One's ethical core is a useful guide.

The implication of the metaphor is that the good guys have a piece of equipment they consult that keeps them going in the right direction. Details regarding this device are hard to come by, but the implication is that bad actors either have a bad one or fail to consult it in times of need. Really good quality moral compasses cannot be ordered online and we too often fail to calibrate our devices.

A compass points to a fixed external reference. Literally, this is a large deposit of iron in the Earth's surface near the North Pole. There is a bit of relativity at work here. Magnetic north has greater power to define a common point the farther away we are from it. A compass is unreliable above 66 degrees latitude north and totally useless at the North Pole. One might say that the closer we are to our moral principles, the more "latitude" we enjoy. The pole star is another metaphor that has the same shortcomings. Those in the Southern Hemisphere are clueless.

Even if the moral compass was in some sense a useful and necessary guide to finding our place in the moral world, it is not sufficient. There is a large gap between knowing where we are and going in the right direction. Some people want to know where north is because they intend to travel east. Even worse, there are those who are interested in orienting themselves in moral space "close enough" to true north so their colleagues will not notice the deviation.

Perhaps a better metaphor is the moral center or core. This is an individually and personally defined reference point, but one that is defined by the totality of relationships with others. It is the definition of our better self. There is no landmark that says "here is my moral core." It can only be inferred from how we habitually relate to those around us. An ethically centered businessman or businesswoman maximizes profits consistent with enforceable social norms and laws. An ethically centered academic refrains from building his or her reputation on claims known to be misleading. An ethically centered oral health professional maximizes oral health, subject to certain constraints of safety and profit.

Unlike the moral compass that works best for extremely distant orientation and is only suggestive, the moral core is most practical close to home. When the core is off-center, it creates friction every time we move. Ethical misalignment is unsustainable.

It is nice to teach and cite abstract ethical principles and to pass out moral compasses. The real work is done, however, by aligning our moral centers so as to optimize the benefit and minimize the damage to our relationships with others. ■

Quacks, Charlatans and the Hippocratic Oath

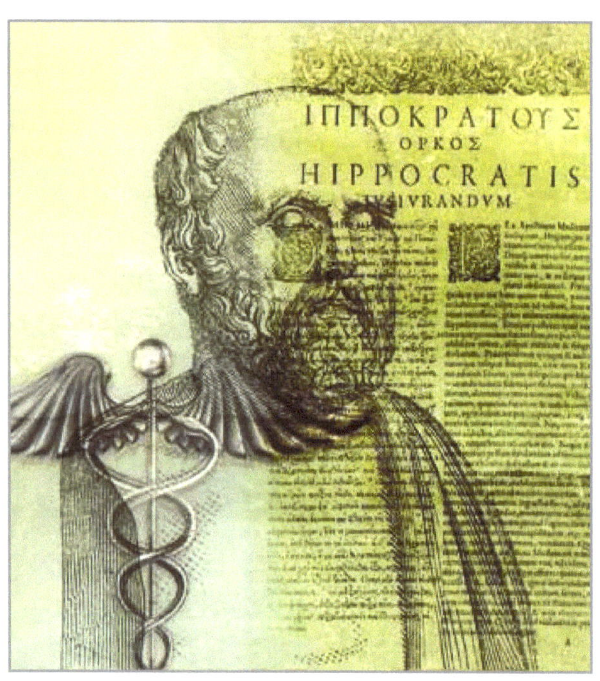

The nub:

1. "First, do not harm" is a pseudo-ethical principle.

2. Quacks cause harm; charlatans are evil.

3. It is negligent to overlook others causing harm.

Once while lecturing, I mentioned that "first, do no harm" is not found in the Hippocratic Oath. This caused a bit of a distraction when a group in the back huddled around a laptop. Finally, it was exclaimed, quite audibly, "[Expletive deleted], he's right."

Primum non nocere is Latin and those at the Hippocratic School spoke Greek. It appears that "first, do not harm" was introduced by lawyers in the late Middle Ages. The current fashion of connecting the slogan and the Hippocratic Corpus is pseudointellectualism. There is small harm in that.

A reasonable translation of the phrase in question is "I will use my art to help the sick according to my ability and judgment, but never with a view to injury and wrong-doing." The paragraph goes on to give examples of not poisoning people or inducing abortions. The point is essentially that a healer will not use the power of his or her profession for *evil* ends.

The difference between "harm" and "evil" is intent. The difference between manslaughter and murder is intent. "Bad outcomes" (a politically correct term for harms) happen in dentistry, but that is harm without intent.

Quacks are healers who use techniques disapproved of by the established community. Generally, they believe in what they are doing. The Hippocratic School felt all who cut tissue, as for example for relief of gall stones, were outside the profession. All dentists would have been regarded as quacks.

Charlatans, on the other hand, know they are causing harm. That makes them evil. Dentists who overtreat or fraudulently bill are charlatans.

It is evil to persist in a practice when expected harm has been pointed out, to avoid reasonable investigation to determining whether harm is likely or to pass silently by as others are causing harm.

Quacks advertise the practices they believe (but the rest of us doubt) will be of benefit to patients. Charlatans hide their harmful work. So information plays a different role in these two cases. Confronting bad actors with the evidence that their behavior is damaging should help in the former case but not the latter.

Failure to take corrective action in the face of valid evidence of harm is an ethical shortcoming. It is called negligence. An unrepentant quack is negligent. Failure to provide that evidence when we know what quacks are doing to patients is also negligence. It is unethical to ignore quacks.

Confronting charlatans is another matter. The most predictable effect is to drive the bad acting underground. Communication is cut off by denial; corrective action is avoided as being less in the charlatan's interest than continuing to misbehave. Information is not the answer here. The system of rewards and punishments must be altered to favor doing what is right. And it is negligent for the profession not to do so. ■

Getting Rights Right

The nub:

1. Lay state representatives grant licenses; organized dentistry grants membership.

2. Legal and moral rights are different and cannot be substituted for each other.

3. The moral can influence the legal but not substitute for it (and vice versa).

Somebody told me years ago that just because somebody has a right to do something does not mean it is right for him or her to do it. We are free to do many stupid things. A dentist who believes his or her colleague is practicing below the standard of care has a right to notify some party within organized dentistry to say so. (The ADA code of professional conduct says a dentist in such a position MUST do so. As far as I know, no dentist has ever been removed from organizational membership for failing to do so. The California Dental Association Code of Ethics does not contain this provision.)

The difference between having a right and doing what is right comes down to the ground on which one makes a stand.

Licensure: Dentists practice on a license to provide commercial services to the public in a safe and nondiscriminatory fashion. State attorneys general manage licenses consistent with statutes and regulations voted by legislatures and enforce these through investigatory mechanisms and state dental boards (or state comprehensive health professional boards).

Professional membership: Two-thirds of dentists belong to organized dentistry. This is a voluntary membership that includes a promise to abide by a code of professional conduct. Typically, the code contains behavior concerning relationships among professionals who are not part of licensure and a clause saying that all members must also abide by civil laws and licensure requirements in the appropriate jurisdictions.

There are separate standards, investigation and informants and penalties for licensure and for voluntary membership. In some states, judicial councils, or some such body, will function in parallel with state licensure enforcement but each has a separate standing. One can remove a practitioner's license; the other can remove a practitioner's membership in the voluntary organization. The recent U.S. Supreme Court decision regarding the role of the state dental board in North Carolina explicitly recognized the ADA code. It praised the association for calling for high standards and specifically stated that the code had no legal status with respect to licensure.

There is a moral side to the issue as well. There, one stands on what is right (ethically appropriate). Sometimes, the best thing to do is sit down with a colleague whose behavior is damaging patients and the profession. The ultimate authority in this case is the ethical convictions of two moral agents. (It is unfair and unwise to go into these matters assuming one is ethical and the other is not.) The collective wisdom of the profession on how to practice is a powerful resource, even though it lacks legal standing. But there is a danger there. Trial in the court of public opinion or rumor discipline is immoral and may even be legally actionable. ■

How to Spot an Ethical Problem

The nub:

1. Ethical issues cannot be resolved by facts or reason.
2. Deciding what you want to do and then looking for a justification is easy, but it is not ethics.
3. Potential ethical issues can be avoided by ignoring others' values.

Is the decision to prophylactically remove third molars an ethical issue? What about insurance plans that limit the frequency of periodontal treatments, a single standard of care for patients regardless of their level of cooperation, public water fluoridation or where one locates a dental practice? Are they ethical issues? Those questions were selected because they are not addressed by the ADA or CDA codes and because multiple and conflicting principles from dentistry and others from ethics generally can be used to give different answers. So are they really ethical issues?

Strange to say, ethics experts have tended to focus more on looking for situations (often small and trivial ones) where their theories or principles apply than on clarifying the boundaries between ethical behavior and actions that can safely be taken without having to worry about the ethical dimensions. The hottest topic in professional ethics today is "trollyology." Should you push a fat man off an overpass to slow down or stop an out-of-control trolley headed toward five folks tied to the tracks ahead? If all the papers written on the topic were dropped on the tracks, they would probably stop the trolley.

Here is my take on how to spot an ethical issue. If my action affects others and the other person's actions affect me, we might have an ethical problem. It is further required that our disagreement about what is mutually best cannot entirely be resolved by appeal to fact or by either acting alone.

Some dentists prefer aggressive and some conservative approaches to TMJ problems; some believe that early orthodontic treatment is unsound because it adds cost and does not change outcomes; some dentists are alarmed over amalgam. Holding these opinions or even writing and speaking about them occasionally under an ethical flag is most often attempted by talking to a friendly crowd instead of those affected. But if all those with a stake in our proposed actions are not part of the conversation, we still do not have an ethical issue.

When the others involved are patients, the ethical issue is typically one of sharing information, because there is a large overlap in the goals of dentists and patients. When informed consent is disguised as "hold-harmless" language instead of an invitation to explore joint actions, this is legal territory, not ethical. When facts are shared but differences remain to be worked out, ethics begins.

One way to cheat in ethics is to say that others' values are wrong. If our facts are not convincing, we paint others as ignorant, stubborn or watching the wrong TV channel. Sometimes in frustration with the seeming impossibility of bringing others around to our values by telling them our side, we simply say their values do not really matter. ■

Does Fluoride Poison Red Herrings?

The nub:

1. Making perfection a requirement means missing out on the best available.

2. It is misleading to choose between available alternatives and impossible ones.

3. The market for red herrings is much higher than it should be at the moment.

Some of the public's reasoning about oral health is distorted. The profession has an ethical duty to try to straighten this out, individually and as policy.

Problem: How does a public official block a proposal that has every prospect of doing some good for the citizens they represent? Solution: Suggest an alternative and then act on it as if doing one precludes doing the other.

At a city council meeting, council members voted to send a letter requesting that the city be exempt from state policy regarding water fluoridation. The city elders did not want to appear to be swayed by the parade of scary people who were convinced that the whole world is a conspiracy, but the two dentists who spoke presented "inconvenient" arguments in favor of fluoride. One dentist explained how fluoridation would reduce the number of lost school days. With a state "average daily attendance" funding mechanism for schools, this works out to fluoridation returning about $2.5 million per year to the county where this "troublesome" discussion occurred.

Taking a bottle of soda from under the dais, a council member explained that getting kids to cut down on soft drinks would make even greater improvements in oral health. This tactic is known as a red herring argument. (It also has some nice overtones of blaming the victim.) When riding to the hounds was the thing in England, the most sporting gentlemen gave the fox a chance by dragging strong smelling fish, such as a red herring, across likely trails to confuse the dogs. Thus, a red herring argument substitutes another important problem for a workable but unpopular one.

The fallacy involves an apparently well-intended person seeming to make a rational choice between two alternatives: removing fluoride or removing soda. The illusion is that two alternatives are never on the table at the same time. Good logic would have dictated that the council member should have introduced a motion to spend $2.5 million each year to get children to drink less soda.

When dentists buy supplies or patients select treatments, they must consider both the benefits of each ingredient and the packages they come in. We cannot force all the benefits into a single product (low price, perfect safety, complete efficacy). We have to make our choices between the packages, not the ingredients in ideal combination. The policy we should choose is the one that is best for most, despite the fact that it still has some shortcomings. ■

Multiple Fee Schedules

The nub:

1. Value of services is determined by patients and payers, not by dentists.

2. Cost of providing acceptable care to all patients is determined by dentists.

3. Dentistry works when the fully informed and uncoerced value to patients and cost to dentists are aligned.

What a mess! A crown for this patient can be billed at $1,200 because she is highly motivated and fee for service. The same crown for another patient is $820, but the patient is balking at the copay. If the eligibility period is jiggered, the situation might be improved. A Medicaid patient may not have any third-party assistance or personal means of affording badly needed treatment. All of the patients may benefit to the same extent from a crown, and of course the quality of work and attending treatment support must be identical in every case. Surely, there must be an ethical issue here somewhere.

Sometimes we try to solve these problems based on these assumptions: Patients value treatment exactly the same way dentists do and "somebody" is supposed to be providing sufficient funds to keep dentists gainfully employed according to their standards. The polar-opposite position is equally indefensible. Dentistry is not a free-market commodity because patients are not fully informed and uncoerced actors and oral health burdens are borne to some extent by society as a whole.

Here is a true story that may help untangle this. When I was a new faculty member at UOP in 1972, Dean Dr. Dale Redig sent me down to the Stanford Business School to see if we could get a little consulting help. I met with Dr. James March, a paragon in business decision-making. I tentatively inquired about fees and Dr. March quoted what at the time was unthinkable: $700 per hour.

He recognized my consternation and gave me a three-minute business lesson that was worth well more than $700. He said he would offer the same advice to General Motors or the Palo Alto YMCA. It would be a bargain for the big car manufacturer and a bad investment for the YMCA. Lesson: The value of any service is determined by the consumer.

Dentists are justified in offering their professional services at any price they deem appropriate, provided that it is the same price and quality to all patients. Patients are entitled to make an informed and uncoerced choice about receiving care. Patients will value identical care differently based on their personal values, available subsidies and intangibles such as convenience of appointments (which may add hundreds of dollars to the nominal fee). Third parties, such as employers, the government and charitable causes, are justified in tilting the market in favor of certain groups for social effect by adding money for target groups.

What is not ethical is to cherry-pick patients or mislead them in an effort to "work around" what dentists may regard as insufficient funds for the kind of work they would like to do or to overtreat and overcharge to make things "fair" for them. ■

The Ethical Safety Net

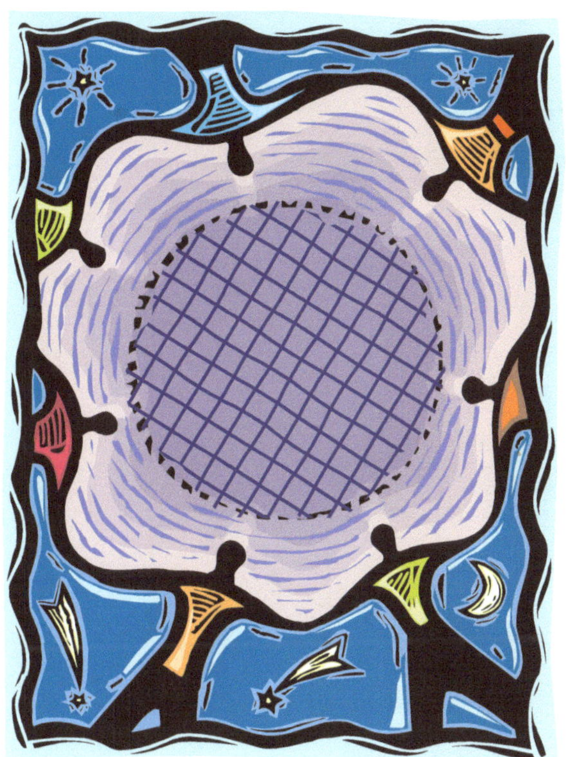

The nub:

1. To avoid the safety net being taken for granted, the unfortunate must have a voice in managing it.

2. Redistribution of wealth seems to increase the productivity of both the most and the least productive.

3. Dentistry will profit from making oral health everyone's responsibility.

There are no human societies that disregard the least fortunate. There are no pure meritocracies that grant a right to keep everything one has earned. There are always quibbles about the details of the redistribution and attempts to separate the "deserving poor" from the "undeserving ones," but creating some minimal floor of resources is what it means to be a social community. Our parents must have had something like this in mind when they sacrificed to help us through our helpless years.

The economist Kenneth Arrow received a Nobel Prize for proving that the social welfare problem, the optimal shape of the safety net, can never be determined to everyone's satisfaction. There has always been debate over the extent to which subsidies dampen the productivity motivation of both those taxed and those receiving subsidies. Studies, such as Frohlich and Oppenheimer's *Choosing Justice: An Experimental Approach to Ethical Theory*, find that groups tend to choose a rule such as "provide for the unfortunate and then the winners can take all they can get." There is virtually no support for the opposite approach of "everyone should get what he or she can and then if there is anything left over, divide it among the unfortunate."

Those who favor a small safety net often argue that "giving things to underperformers promotes dependence." Blanket entitlement certainly has conspicuous drawbacks. But the evidence suggests that helping others gain capacity to help themselves does promote responsibility, while giving them leftovers has the opposite effect. Mission and charity work that makes the unfortunate more employable or keeps children in school longer is the best kind of pro bono dentistry.

A further multiplier for the strength of the safety net is when the unfortunate are given a voice in how the system should work. Research suggests that the largest percent increases in productivity come when the poor participate in building a better system. The best drug counselors are those recovering from addictions.

The reason why the safety net is often laid out in remote locations to which dentists travel is that the relationship involves health care professionals, governments and patients. The great mission programs are partnerships. It is recognized that ministering to the unfortunate is a responsibility of society, not just individual professionals within society. This is a three-part arrangement with roles for everyone. It is a dodge to say "somebody" ought to do something, meaning only one of the three or even any two.

Many in the profession are praiseworthy for their charity work. Typically, this is a small proportion of the profession, although its impact is impressive. In one report, 50% of charity care was delivered by 5% of dentists.

The lesson seems clear: The safety net can be mended from all sides. ■

About the Author

Dr. Chambers is professor of orthodontics and former associate dean for academic affairs and scholarship at the University of the Pacific, Arthur A. Dugoni School of Dentistry in San Francisco. He is also the editor of the American College of Dentists. He has served as a consultant to most national dental organizations and dental schools in the United States and Canada, as well as being an examiner for the Malcolm Baldrige National Quality Award and on the Commission on Dental Accreditation.

He holds EdM, MBA, and PhD degrees and was elected to four national honor societies: (a) Phi Delta Kappa (education) 1969; (b) Beta Gamma Sigma (management) 1979; (c) Omicron Kappa Upsilon (dentistry) 1991; (d) Phi Kappa Phi (arts and sciences) 2000. Dr Chambers has been a visiting scholar in philosophy at Cambridge University, The London School of Economics, and UC Berkeley. He has published over 650 papers, including a monthly column on ethics in the *CDA Journal*.

Dr. Chambers received the American Dental Education Association Gies Award for Achievement in 2018. He has made significant contributions in the areas of humanism in dental education, competency-based education, raising the voice of young professionals, licensure on graduation, and clinical decision making.

www.ingramcontent.com/pod-product-compliance
Lightning Source LLC
Chambersburg PA
CBHW052041190326
41519CB00003BA/247
9780578733845